Advance praise for *The*

James Howard Kunstler plainly has a lot to say about the state of the world. And while much of it is bad, bad news — aggressively, congenitally, perhaps even fatally bad — he speaks with such vim and vigor that you find yourself nodding in agreement rather than looking for a noose. Duncan Crary wrangles these free-wheeling conversations masterfully. A bracing dose of reality for an unreal world.

— Stephen J. Dubner, co-author, *Freakonomics* and *SuperFreakonomics*

James Howard Kunstler is one of the great thinkers of our time. Duncan Crary has compiled a collection of interviews with him that are so enlightening yet casual that the reader feels like they're eavesdropping into the den of Kunstler's prodigious mind.

— Andrew D. Blechman, author, *Leisureville*

Kunstler is the most authoritative, audacious and prescient writer of urbanism in America today. His analysis of the converging factors closing in on cities in the 21st Century is critical to understand the future of America, and its options moving forward. Kunstler understands cities, and the failures of suburban sprawl, like no other. Prepare to be enlightened, infuriated and amused.

— Gregory Greene, Director, *The End of Suburbia*

Jim and Duncan: erudite, eloquent, with the good sense to be living the way they want right now. Here they converse at length and with good humor about the hilariously grotesque North American nightmare of car-addicted suburban sprawl. Make use of their wit and wisdom to plan your escape from it, or sit back and laugh with them if you already have.

— Dmitry Orlov, author, *Reinventing Collapse*
dmitry.orlov@gmail.com

Earlier praise for the KunstlerCast podcast, which this book is based on:

...some of the smartest, most honest urban commentary around—online or off.
— Columbia Journalism Review

...the KunstlerCast delivers the goods, with inspired rants on a variety of subjects related to American places (and non-places) and the coming peak oil reality.

— Treehugger.com

the KUNSTLERCAST:

conversations with JAMES HOWARD KUNSTLER

...the tragic comedy
of urban sprawl

DUNCAN CRARY

NEW SOCIETY PUBLISHERS

Cover design by Diane McIntosh. Art by Ken Avidor.

Printed in Canada. First printing October 2011.

Paperback ISBN: 978-0-86571-693-3   eISBN: 978-1-55092-472-5

Inquiries regarding requests to reprint all or part of *The KunstlerCast* should be addressed to New Society Publishers at the address below.

To order directly from the publishers, please call toll-free (North America) 1-800-567-6772, or order online at www.newsociety.com

Any other inquiries can be directed by mail to:

New Society Publishers
P.O. Box 189, Gabriola Island, BC V0R 1X0, Canada   (250) 247-9737

New Society Publishers' mission is to publish books that contribute in fundamental ways to building an ecologically sustainable and just society, and to do so with the least possible impact on the environment, in a manner that models this vision. We are committed to doing this not just through education, but through action. The interior pages of our bound books are printed on Forest Stewardship Council® acid-free paper that is **100% post-consumer recycled** (100% old growth forest-free), processed chlorine free, and printed with vegetable-based, low-VOC inks, with covers produced using FSC® stock. New Society also works to reduce its carbon footprint, and purchases carbon offsets based on an annual audit to ensure a carbon neutral footprint. For further information, or to browse our full list of books and purchase securely, visit our website at: www.newsociety.com

LIBRARY AND ARCHIVES CANADA CATALOGUING IN PUBLICATION

Kunstler, James Howard
The KunstlerCast : conversations with James Howard Kunstler /
[interviewed by] Duncan Crary.

Includes index.
ISBN 978-0-86571-693-3

1. Kunstler, James Howard—Interviews. 2. Authors, American—20th century—Interviews. 3. Sociology, Urban—United States. I. Crary, Duncan II. Title.

HT119.K85 2011   307.760973   C2011-905948-7

NEW SOCIETY PUBLISHERS
www.newsociety.com

MIX
Paper from
responsible sources
FSC® C016245

For Grace and John Crary

Special thanks to
Eileen Sheehan, Roger Noyes, Philip Schwartz,
Ian and Craig White, Peter Albrecht, Tom Reynolds,
Ingrid Witvoet, Alison Bates, Jes Constantine, Ben McGrath,
Matt Dellinger, Andrew Blechman, Wendy Anthony,
the Congress for the New Urbanism and our listeners.

Contents

I lived in lies all my life,
And I've been living here for a long, long time,
I know it's been coming down a while now.
> —John J McCauley III, Deer Tick
> "Art Isn't Real (City of Sin)"

THERE'S A PASSAGE in *Moby-Dick* where Herman Melville compares two lone whaling ships crossing the Pacific to strangers crossing the "illimitable Pine Barrens of New York State." If these travelers were to encounter each other in such inhospitable wilds, he explains, it would be natural for them to give "mutual salutation" and stop for a while to interchange their news of the world. In whaling argot, this is called a "gam."

More than a century and a half has passed since Melville wrote those words, and little remains of the illimitable Pine Barrens he described on the outskirts of Albany. But the place has become a new kind of wilderness that is equally inhospitable to this traveler. It is a terrain of parking lots, shopping malls, subdivisions and highways. It is a geography of nowhere that stretches from the edge of my town to yours. But we will not be adrift here alone forever.

Kunstler will be here soon. And when he arrives, we'll have ourselves a gam.

Intro

JAMES HOWARD KUNSTLER has been called a lot of things. The world's most outspoken critic of suburban sprawl. A caustic hero of New Urbanism. A peak oil provocateur. Curmudgeon. Jeremiah. Doomer. Dystopian. Generalist. Social critic. Crank.

He usually just goes by Jim.

My first encounter with Jim was through *The Geography of Nowhere*, a highly acclaimed, landmark polemic about the failures of suburbia. I was nineteen when I discovered that book, just a few years after its 1993 publication. And I've been amusing, enlightening and pissing people off with what I found between its covers ever since.

Like so many of my Generation X, I was hatched on a cul-de-sac in the American suburbs. As an adolescent, I grew deeply dissatisfied with that mode of living. It was monotonous, ugly and isolating, and I was acting out along with my peers in strange and bad ways. But it wasn't until *Geography* that I acquired the tools to be able to articulate the things I found profoundly wrong about the non-place of suburbia. Kunstler's acid wit was a laxative to my constipated feelings about our everyday surroundings. He seemed to put across, in a wickedly funny manner, all of the complaints and disappointments and frustrations that had been a lump in my throat for years. I knew suburbia sucked. What I lacked until I saw it in print was the vocabulary and framework that JHK used to back up the sentiment. I was never the same again.

Kunstler wrote other books addressing the subject, and I read them, too. In *Home From Nowhere* he introduced me to the New Urbanism, a reformist movement of architects and planners working to create spaces you could actually give a damn about. In *The City in Mind*, he dissected the urban organism with eight portraits of major world cities—some wonderful, some utterly unsustainable. These follow-up titles never garnered the same attention as the first, but they helped secure his place on the totem pole of urban thinkers. He was clearly doing for a new generation what Jane Jacobs had done for hers. People across the nation were taking notice.

By the time *City* hit the shelves in 2002, I was no longer a passive reader of Kunstler's work. I was actually following in his footsteps. I had landed a dreary gig as a reporter covering the municipal meetings and so-called quality of life issues in a suburb of Albany, New York. This happened to be in the same town where Jim himself had toiled as a reporter thirty years earlier, when his lens on suburbia had its first real grinding. He left the area after that for a stint at *Rolling Stone* and a few other bohemian adventures, but ultimately returned to settle in nearby Saratoga Springs, where he's lived ever since. Lucky for me, that made JHK a local source that I could call upon for an occasional quote about various sprawl-building efforts in my beat. And I took whatever chance I got to insert his voice into my reporting, planting little Kunstler bombs to be delivered to the doorsteps of suburbia by way of a newsprint Trojan horse. (That's how I imagined it at the time.... I was twenty-three.)

I graduated to other papers, magazines and projects. But I kept returning to Kunstler. I felt compelled to bring his ideas to new audiences, whether they wanted to hear them or not. There were other contrarians out there challenging the suburban dogmas of the day, but in my mind JHK was the best in the genre. His rhetoric was meme-spreading, widely repeated and often imitated. Sure, he cussed and used hyperbole and had a malicious sense of humor. He was funny as hell. But he was not just arming the populace with zingers to hurl at defective planners, brain-dead architects and evil developers. He was shifting the public consensus by getting us regular folks to think about the places where we spend our lives. That's how you reclaim the public realm. And it's that empowering aspect of his thought-sharing that I still find most appealing.

In recent years, Kunstler's gaze has turned to a new chapter in the suburban saga: its future. He believes it will soon become self-evident that our zeal to suburbanize this nation—in a seemingly endless cycle of revolving debt— was "the greatest misallocation of resources in the history of the world." The choices we made during the past half-century in how we would inhabit the landscape, conduct commerce and even feed ourselves will prove to be tragic. We made these tragic choices during a "fiesta" of cheap fossil fuel, which is now ending. A permanent energy crisis is upon us, and it is coinciding with a financial collapse that will leave our civilization functionally broke. Our failures in leadership at all levels may bring about political instability. Throw in the unknown effects of climate change and we begin to see a picture of the converging catastrophes of the twenty-first century. Welcome to what Kunstler has dubbed "The Long Emergency," which is also the title of his latest and most provocative nonfiction book.

The worst of car-dependent suburbia is "toast," in Kunstler's prognosis. We won't have the will or the finances to retrofit it. And so it is destined to be "a living arrangement with no future," he says. Fortunately, the New Urbanists accomplished something very important during the fiasco of suburban build-out that will prove invaluable in the times to come. They retrieved from cultural oblivion the important principles and practices of tradition-rooted architecture and urban design. Soon, Kunstler predicts, this body of pre-automobile place-making skills will be applied once again to our smaller cities and villages as we rediscover and reinhabit them. Agriculture, commerce, daily life will be conducted locally again in a more organic arrangement. There will be resistance and pushback to these inevitable changes. But eventually, JHK is serenely convinced, we will find ourselves a much happier people, living in a more rewarding setting.

There's a lot more to Kunstler's worldview, which is often misunderstood or digested only in bits and pieces through brief media appearances. Even his followers tend to compartmentalize him. Many of those who know him through his earlier critiques of suburbia are somewhat put off by his more recent preoccupation with peak oil, financial collapse and crystal ball-gazing. On the other hand, a lot of the "collapsniks" who found him through *The*

Long Emergency and his *Clusterfuck Nation* blog are somewhat bored by and dismissive of his urbanist thoughts. Neither camp seems to appreciate the full spectrum of "Kunstler's Unified Field Theory of Modern Civilization," as another reporter once described it to me. To be honest, I didn't get the whole picture myself. Which is why I felt it was time to sit Jim in front of a microphone and start from the beginning.

By 2007 I had gotten into a new media form called podcasting, which is really just a means of delivering old-fashioned talk radio through the Internet. I was producing a monthly podcast for a think tank promoting the philosophy of humanism, which I took as another chance to speak with Kunstler about the need for a more credible "human habitat." His appearance on that program was well received and we seemed to have a good "on-air" chemistry. So we decided to keep meeting—in his house in Saratoga, in my apartment in Troy, sometimes in the field—to record more conversations for an independent side project we called "The KunstlerCast," for lack of a better name. It was a weekly discussion about "the tragic comedy of suburban sprawl," an endless source of material for Kunstler's dyspeptic commentary.

For many, it was an addictive little program. Jim had the gift of gab, which is not always the case with writers. He feared no topic, needed little to get him going, and everything he said was off the top of his head. My most important contribution was probably showing up to press "record," though I did help to keep him on track. I assumed the role of host, and sometimes foil, to his magnificent rants. My intention was to be a proxy for the audience who could enjoy Jim's snark from the safety of their earbuds. I was always more interested in learning from Jim rather than interviewing him, and our listeners seemed to enjoy that dynamic. It's a very traditional thing to do, to sit with an "elder" and receive the transfer of knowledge from one generation to the next. We just happened to have ten thousand iPods sitting alongside us.

Kunstler is a lightning rod, though, and if you stand close to a lightning rod you'll eventually get zapped. Over the years I received my share of criticism for my performance, in a way that only the Internet would allow. I was called "kind of a dork," "a doting young host" and "a satirical, smirking sidekick." One fan of the show accused me of lobbing softball questions.

At times, even Jim could be a little imperious in his tone with me, especially early on. It is no secret among those who have interviewed him that Kunstler can be a challenging subject; the adjective I hear most often is "prickly." He has little patience for combative questioning or lines that attempt to lead him to a conclusion he hasn't drawn. He doesn't take kindly to being chastised for not being hopeful enough or for not proffering enough "solutions." But overall he was patient, kind and generous with me and I quickly found that he is more than willing to assess his own ideas and limitations. All I needed to do was simply nudge him toward those topics and get out of the way.

For four years, I talked with a very interesting man named James Howard Kunstler. This is a record of what he told me.

—DC

A Technical Note

When I first conceived of the idea to produce a book based on a podcast, I thought I had invented the world's laziest way to write a book. My idea was: stick a microphone in front of a well-known author, record, transcribe and publish. What follows was not so easy to produce. And it is not a verbatim transcript of my conversations with Jim.

This is an edited reconstruction of a dialogue that spanned many years. It is based on transcripts of our weekly dispatches, which unfolded in no particular order, so I have selected, reordered and edited for length and clarity the exchanges I felt were most important. With a few slight exceptions, I have left Jim's words as they were spoken, cutting only for length, redundancy and to splice related thoughts together. I have taken more liberty with my own words, mostly to provide smoother transitions.

It is a strange thing to be credited as the author of a book based on a long conversation in which another person does most of the talking. I am more like the host of this book, which eventually wrote itself.

Chapter 1: The Geography of Nowhere

The Glossary of Nowhere

Duncan Crary: I was rereading the opening to *The Geography of Nowhere* recently. Not much has changed since you wrote that eighteen years ago.

James Howard Kunstler: I've changed though. My brain has shrunk from too many off-gassing carpets.

DC: You said you wrote that book to give people a vocabulary to talk about their unhappiness with suburbia, because it's so hard to articulate some of these feelings.

JHK: I was struggling with it myself. I went through a period—ten, fifteen

years before I wrote that book—of trying to formulate a vocabulary for myself to understand it. I made several attempts to produce written essays on the subject. And I found myself repeatedly defeated, largely because, like a lot of other normal people who are affected by this, I kept defaulting to these style issues.

I didn't quite understand the physical form and design issues. It wasn't until I encountered Christopher Alexander and Andrés Duany and many other contemporaries

1

Scary Places

Eighty percent of everything ever built in America has been built in the last fifty years, and most of it is depressing, brutal, ugly, unhealthy, and spiritually degrading—the jive plastic computer tract home wastelands, the Potemkin village shopping plazas with their vast parking lagoons, the Lego-block hotel complexes, the "gourmet mansardic" junk-food joints, the Orwellian office "parks" featuring buildings sheathed in the same reflective glass as the sunglasses worn by chain-gang guards, the particle board garden apartments rising up in every meadow and cornfield, the freeway loops around every big and little city with their clusters of discount merchandise marts, the whole destructive, wasteful, toxic, agoraphobia-inducing spectacle that politicians proudly call "growth."

The newspaper headlines may shout about global warming, extinctions of living species, the devastations of rain forests, and other worldwide catastrophes, but Americans evince a striking complacency when it comes to their everyday environment and the growing calamity that it represents.

I had a hunch that many other people find their surroundings as distressing as I do my own, yet I sense too that they lack the vocabulary to understand what's wrong with the places they ought to know best. And that is why I wrote this book.

—James Howard Kunstler
The Geography of Nowhere[1]

in the field that I began to really understand what I was talking about.

DC: You take these topics seriously. But so much of what you write about suburban sprawl and modern architecture is funny. Your speaking engagements are especially funny when you use images to illustrate your point—like, you'll describe some modernist building in Schenectady, New York as "Darth Vader's Helmet" and of course, with the photo of this weird curvy glass building on the screen, the audience goes wild.[2]

JHK: Yeah, it's sort of evolved into a comedy act. But I was a theater student in college—that was my major, believe it or not—and I was exposed to Samuel Beckett at a tender age. Beckett put it very well: "Nothing is funnier than unhappiness."[3] These environments cause us so much unhappiness, so much distress, that they're a source of comedy.

When you see a Laurel and Hardy comedy from the 1920s—these two morons hitting each other with two-by-fours and dropping pianos on each other—or even a Tweety Bird cartoon, what we're seeing is people hurting each other. But we laugh. Getting hit by a two- by-four in reality is not a pleasant thing. In fact, it can kill you. When you see it on stage or in a film, though, it becomes funny because we identify with the pain of it. So the pain of our everyday environments in America is so extreme—they're so bad, they suck so egregiously—that all that's left, finally, is humor.

DC: Let's go through some of the funnier terms and phrases in your "Glossary of Nowhere" that you use to talk about suburbia. You can explain what they mean and where they came from. What are "parking lagoons?"

JHK: That one was a little ironic, because the word "lagoon" evokes a lovely kind of tropical place that you'd like to hang around on your yacht. Whereas the parking lot is the opposite—it's a demoralizing, repellent place. I was just trying to mess with people a little bit.

DC: You can park your yacht-sized car in the parking lot, though.

JHK: That was an implication.

DC: You have a lot of riffs on parking lots. For one of the bits in your spiel you'll put up a slide of a parking lot that's so huge you can't see the Walmart from the Target store on the other side because the curvature of the Earth blocks your view.

JHK: Right. The scale of the streets and the parking lots is so huge that you end up feeling like you're in a surrealist painting where you can't find the horizon. You're lost in space out there. And to be lost in space is extremely distressing. One of the reasons that urban design depends on defining space well is that people don't like to be lost in space. They like to know where they are. They like to know where things begin and end.

DC: Speaking of being lost in space, how about UFOs? You refer to a lot of modern buildings as UFOs.

JHK: I may have gotten that from somebody else, although I have no recollection of who it might have been. The whole idea was the development as UFO landing strip, and the idea that you're actually not building anything memorable— you're just building a place for something out-of-this-world to put down on. The trouble is, once these UFOs land, they don't fly away.

DC: You've also noticed that these UFOs tend to bring a lot of juniper shrubs with them. In the talk you gave at the TED conference, you showed the audience a photo of a street with a bark mulch bed and three weird-looking juniper shrubs, which you described as the mother ship, R2D2 and C3PO.[4]

JHK: Yeah, it was a big juniper shrub and two little junior ones exploring the planet to see if they could colonize it. They were doing a chemical analysis of the bark mulch to see if they could live there.

That was a comment on the idiocy of our landscaping design, which tends to be used as a Nature Band-Aid to mitigate the failures of our architecture.

DC: That's another signature expression of yours: "Nature Band-Aid."

JHK: The reason why you see so many stupid landscaping fantasies around American cities and suburbs is because our buildings are so bad we're constantly trying to hide them behind beds of shrubs and crabapple trees. You have a mutilated town, with terrible buildings that have been built in the last thirty years—the Burger Kings and all that—and we think that if we stick a little bark mulch bed with juniper shrubs in front of them, that it makes it OK. We have no confidence in our ability to create urban places, so "nature" is always the default cure.

We also do it to make ourselves feel better about being "green." You know: "I'm green. I'm a good person, with good intentions." The whole thing has been a complete waste of time and money and effort. If we put up buildings that were worth looking at in the first place, we wouldn't need the Nature Band-Aids.

What you're also seeing is a very deep typological confusion over what is inherently urban and what is rural—between what is in the town, and what is in the country, and what belongs where. Typically, what this involves is people trying to "ruralize" the city. If your city is bad, you try to cure it by bringing the country into the city. And what we've demonstrated in about fifty years of doing this is that it's no cure at all—in fact, it only makes things worse.

An interesting exercise, for those who still do foreign travel: go to the plaza in front of the Pantheon in Rome. It's a nicely proportioned outdoor public room, with walls that are composed of the sides of the buildings around it. There's probably not one green thing within the whole ensemble except maybe one flower box. They understand, in these other countries, that you don't have to "green" everything up. The architecture itself does the work of being wonderful.

DC: I used to cover the planning board meetings of a real sprawly suburban town for the newspaper. And these planning board people were obsessed with berms. Everything had to be hidden behind a grassy mound.

JHK: Sure. You just put a bunch of birch trees on a raised esker that runs between the K-Mart and the Walmart and that's supposed to make things all right.

DC: There's something else we try to hide our buildings behind, and it's my favorite expression of yours: "patriotic totems."

JHK: I usually apply that to flagpoles. The reason we see an ensemble of flags flying over the Denny's restaurants is not because they really give a damn about the war in whatever country we're in at the moment. The flags are totems warding off criticism. Because if you put a flag in front of something, that brands it as being something you identify your culture with. You're not supposed to dis your own culture. So that's why there are so many flags in front of the corporate box stores—it allows them to put up crappy buildings that can't be criticized.

DC: "The Fossil Fuel Fiesta"?

JHK: That's what I call the post–World War II era. That was the height of the cheap oil and cheap natural gas fiesta, and it allowed this hypertrophic growth of our cities and the suburban asteroid belts that grew up around them. And it allowed us to create our Happy Motoring Program.

DC: What's the "Happy Motoring Program?"

JHK: That's what we've got in America for gettin' around. You know the thing is, it must have started out as a wonderful experience. Imagine being in the United States in 1927 when there were only a few million cars in the country and the open road was really the open road. The countryside had not been screwed up with all of this stuff. Of course, we had our own oil supply in this country then and it was really cheap. It must have been fabulous.

But that's not the experience of our generations, yours and mine. We got all of the post–World War II crap that changed everything. Happy Motoring was a system that got totally out of control. And now it's nearing its end. We can't imagine living without it and the whole thing is just tragic and awful.

I think it's important to make the point that the whole Happy Motoring Program was not a diabolical scheme worked up by the Devil to make the American people unhappy. It really seemed like it would be a great thing in the early decades and people were rightfully enthusiastic about it. They just couldn't tell how out of control it would get. It's sad.

DC: The Happy Motoring Program is what turned America into our "National Automobile Slum."

JHK: Exactly.

DC: Where did you get "Happy Motoring" from? Did you come up with that?

JHK: No. It was a slogan they used to put on the side of the old Esso gasoline stations—a big thing spelled out in sculpted letters that said "Happy Motoring."

DC: And you like to use it ironically?

JHK: Well, it appeals to me, because it's such a contradiction from what it really evolved into, which is unhappy motoring. And it's going to become increasingly unhappy for a lot of people as they become foreclosed from the Happy Motoring Program.

DC: You refer to a lot of things as "programs" and "projects," including the "Project of Civilization." Why do you refer to civilization as a "project"?

JHK: It is a project in the sense that what we bring to it is purposeful.

DC: And I suppose projects do tend to have a beginning, a middle and an end.

JHK: There's that, too.

DC: How about "techno-grandiosity" and "techno-triumphalism"?

JHK: That's the idea that you can solve absolutely every problem in the world by pushing a computer mouse around—"Dude, we've got technology!" It's a form of self-delusion that we'll be able to keep running everything the way we have during the last sixty years of the cheap energy era. The companion term I use is "techno-rapture."

DC: Anyone who gets an email from you will notice the signature ends with "It's All Good." Where did you pick that up?

JHK: I've attracted a certain number of correspondents over the years. There was this one particular guy—

a reader, who I still correspond with regularly after ten years. He's a very interesting cat. He's a Vietnam veteran, Zen master kind of personality and he introduced me to the saying "It's All Good." He meant it ironically. I took it that way, and I thought it was funny. It just seemed to be about the best way to sum up the American experience of our time.

The Human Habitat

Spiritual Ownership of Place

Any place you allow the car to dominate, the buildings will invariably end up turning their backs to that corridor. All these things add up to make it a place that nobody really wants to be in. Nobody wants to take spiritual ownership of that corridor. All that's left are the commercial considerations about getting attention for what product you're selling—whether it's pancakes or mufflers. There's no consideration for anything else, and in fact we cease to care.

—James Howard Kunstler, May 6, 2010
KunstlerCast #110: "Human Scale"

Duncan Crary: I know you didn't coin it, but the first time I came across the phrase "human habitat" was in *The Geography of Nowhere*. And it struck me. Because we typically only hear the word "habitat" when environmentalists are talking about *wildlife habitat*—the loss of it, usually.

We don't think about our own built environment as being a "habitat." We don't think about the destruction we do to our own habitat. But humans need good habitat, too, in order to be happy and healthy and successful. Just like other animals.

James Howard Kunstler: You're making an interesting point. And I think it shows one of the real shortcomings of the environmental movement in our time. Environmentalists haven't paid enough attention to the human habitat per se or the idea that it's part of the larger ecology of the planet—that it's justified in its existence.

This may reflect their horror at the poor job we've done in elaborating the human habitat during our time of industrial technology. We've taken the human habitat to a scale that's terrible and destroyed an awful lot of other habitats along the way. It's understandably appalling. But the most painful thing for me is that I'm constantly rubbing elbows with real high-toned environmentalists, and to an individual they are absolutely preoccupied with finding some snazzy new way to run their cars. I give lectures at colleges and around the country, and they come up to me afterwards and they tell me that they just got a Prius, you know? They want me to give them a brownie point, or put a medal on them. They don't seem to have any sense of consequence about what this actually leads to.

These people want to live at the end of a twenty-mile dirt road connected to their society by the umbilical cord of their car. By the way, this is characteristic of one of the most famous alternative motoring projects in America, which is Amory Lovins' Hypercar project at his Rocky

Mountain Institute. Here you have a guy running this environmental institute—this guy who's regarded as one of the great geniuses of his generation, Amory Lovins—and he spent fifteen years developing this project to design a car that gets such supernaturally wonderful mileage that it'll be just the greatest thing ever. He never realizes that the main unintended consequence of all this is that it just promotes the idea that we can continue being car-dependent. It shows how cracked we are.

DC: There's all this talk about electric cars and hydrogen fuel cell cars and super-efficient cars. But I don't even care if the fuel you're running your car on is spewing out some kind of fumes that are *good* for the environment. Because I don't want to live in a world where I have to drive my car everywhere—no matter what it runs on. If we do come up with some magic fuel to power everyone's SUV, then we're still stuck in this suburban dystopia where you have to drive to get to work, drive to go shopping, drive to go for a hike....

JHK: The way you've defined the problem is actually another layer that's much more important: if we enabled ourselves to drive our cars for another hundred years we'd completely destroy North America, not to mention the rest of the planet.

The problem in America is not that we're driving the wrong kind of cars. The trouble is we're driving every kind of car incessantly. And we've got to find a way out of the incessant motoring—not a punishing way to live without it, but a happy way to live without it. And it means a completely different paradigm for everyday life.

We would benefit a lot more if environmentalists would put a fraction of their mental energy into thinking about walkable communities or into retrieving really good urban design, or if they put a tenth of their energy into the real important project that we face as far as transportation is concerned, which is restoring the American passenger rail system at all levels—that's what we need the environmental people to put their energy into instead of spending all their time thinking about how we're going to run cars differently. It's totally insane.

DC: Let the car die.

JHK: Let the car die. Let the motoring system die, and let's move on to the next thing—which ought to be good urbanism, walkable neighborhoods, walkable cities that are scaled to the true energy resources of the future, not just wishes and fantasies.

DC: But even the environmentalists have fallen into the trap of suburban thinking.

JHK: Absolutely. This gets to another thing that is essential about understanding the problem of suburbia. The great promise of the suburban venture, and one of the reasons that the environmentalist community is suckered into it, is that it promises to allow you to live an urban life in a rural setting. One of the things this represents is the fact that we have absolutely no faith in our ability to create urban environments at all. Our ability to create cities is so bad— our cities suck so badly, they're so unrewarding, they're so ugly, they're so poorly organized, they're so unintegrated, they're so psychologically defeating, they generate so much anxiety and depression—that the default remedy for this is "nature." So now we have to live in some cartoon version of "the country."

We don't even want to think about what a good human construct could be. So we put absolutely no effort into understanding how to do this. That's one of the reasons the environmental movement has been completely uninterested in urban design per se, because the human habitat doesn't interest them.

DC: Well if we'd paid more attention to our own habitat, if we hadn't abandoned our cities and villages to suburbanize the continent, then maybe we wouldn't need an environmental movement to protect nature from us in the first place.

JHK: Right. But in order to prompt people to make the choice to want to live in the city or the town, those places have to be wonderful. If the "green people" would become really active in urban design and get good at it, then it's likely that fewer people would take the option of living in suburbia and in the countryside. But they have to reward us hugely. Right now, people in the United States aren't getting rewards for living in urban settings—that's one of the great tragedies in all this.

I'm hammering on the environmentalists here, but I hasten to add: I'm not a neocon. I'm not a Republican. I'm not a reactionary. But one of the things I notice is the environmental community generally tends to view this thing they call the "environment" as having value only for recreation or scenery. They don't even value it for agricultural production.

I think that behavior and ideology is deeply out of sync with what we need to do in this country, which is to recreate a meaningful relationship between urban human habitats and a productive rural landscape. We're going to have to produce our food differently in the future because industrial agriculture is going to fail along with all the other things that are dependent on cheap fossil fuel.

We'll get beyond this, though—not because I'm complaining about it, but because circumstances are now developing that are going to compel us to do things differently. And we will. It's going to change everything about how we live. It's going to change our ethos, and our aesthetic, our value system, and our concept of who and where we are. We're going to be a very different people when we exit the cheap energy era.

I'm convinced that the disorders of the twenty-first century are going to return us to a lot of things that we used to do better, including designing better buildings and better towns.

America's Honeymoon with Cities is Over

Duncan Crary: When did Americans decide that we needed to ditch our cities for suburbia?

James Howard Kunstler: For about a hundred years, before the end of World War II, the American city was a manifestation of the industrial experience. And it produced cities that weren't that pleasant to be in.

It's not just the noise and the dirt and smells and the horror of all that—the scale of it is what really starts to disturb people. All of a sudden factories are no longer just three-hundred-foot long boxes in the middle of the city. With things like electrification and the assembly line, they're now the size of a neighborhood. The automobile was imposed on the city, making it more unpleasant than ever. Then came the Great Depression and World War II, adding another layer of neglect and decay to our cities.

By the time the soldiers come home from World War II, American cities are pretty crummy. What we find is the typical American satanic city of belching smokestacks and smelly factories. You get places like Pittsburgh, which was renowned for having so much smoke in the air it was like twilight all the time.

The whole idea of the mass industrial man, living in the worker tenements which are half a century old and deteriorating—it's sort of a dreary panorama. So the one image of the American city that really becomes universal in the early 1950s is Ralph Kramden's apartment in *The Honeymooners* TV show—this miserable, dark little hole in a box, looking out on this miserable light well and fire escape. That becomes everybody's idea of the city, and they reject it completely. They say, "Forget it! We're moving somewhere else."

The Rush to the Suburbs

JHK: We get this huge demographic shift in the fifties. The cities are being decanted into the suburbs. The process had already begun in the 1920s with the first iterations of suburbia, but the Depression and World War II had stalled us. By the 1950s we were back to it. And we begin to have this land rush into the agricultural hinterlands of the cities, otherwise known as the suburbs.

This is all coinciding with the further development of the automobile and all of its accessories and infrastructure, which is fueled by the continued growth of the world-dominant American oil industry.

DC: People often describe the evacuation of American cities after World War II as "white flight."

JHK: Yeah, although that was only one feature of it. I would submit that the other features I described were more important in the whole process.

DC: OK. But how did racial migrations factor into this story of the city and the suburbs?

JHK: While all these events are unfolding, there are still more things in motion. The invention of the mechanical cotton picker in the South puts an end to sharecropper labor. So you get a lot of southern peasants, many of them black, moving up into the industrial cities looking for opportunities. The opportunities were actually there in the industrial cities in the 1950s and '60s. The factories were still humming. They were still making cars in Detroit and making all of the parts of the cars in Akron and Dayton, etc.

But beginning in the 1970s, those manufacturing jobs started to leave. The industries started to incrementally break down and move away. By the 1970s, '80s, '90s we're starting to develop high levels of unemployment, a lack of education and cultural dislocation in the American inner city. That's pretty much what's left in a lot of the heartland industrial cities in America today. So we call that "urban" now, because everybody else is living in this cartoon of the country known as suburbia.

Disassembling the Urban Organism

DC: What makes suburbia so different from the places we lived in before it?

JHK: One of the chief characteristics of suburbia is its disaggregation—the disassembly of the organs of civic life and then the consequent isolation of them—so that all the people live in one place, all the shopping occurs in another place, the offices are in a third place, the industrial stuff is in the fourth place, and all of it can only be accessed by cars.

DC: So how does a healthy city, or village, or town center function?

JHK: A successful city or town is made up of integral parts. You think of these as the organs of the larger organism of the city or town: the residential organs, where the people live; the commercial organs, where commerce and trade take place; the manufacturing organs; the civic organs, where we have our meeting halls, courthouses and the police station—the cultural organs are the museum and the school, the theater and so forth.

In a successful city, these organs are deployed so that most people can get to them without prosthetic assistance—namely the car—and in a way that allows them to enjoy the journey from one organ to the other. Anybody who's been to a European city understands this, because they didn't throw their cities away the way we did. Rome, Florence, Paris, Munich—you go around these places and the journey from point A to point B is very rewarding. You're seeing things that were created deliberately to be beautiful, to reward the human spirit. And you don't have to cross an eight-lane freeway, generally, to get from one to the other.

The main characteristic of a healthy urban organism is that it is scaled to the energy diet that is available to it. Unfortunately, much of the twentieth century provided America with an energy diet that was abnormal. It was the height of the cheap oil and cheap natural gas fiesta, and it allowed us to create urban organisms that were scaled to dimensions that can't be sustained after the peak of the oil era, that arc of decline we're now entering.

Disaggregation and Deadness

We have choices in the designs that we choose for our habitations. Those designs either invoke an idea of aliveness or invoke an idea of deadness. Mostly we've made the choice for deadness in America, and the deadness mostly comes from cutting one thing off from another.

The aliveness comes from when things have transitions between each other that are graceful, beautiful transitions that allow you to go seamlessly from one activity to another, or from one place to another, or from one room to another.

But when you start putting up barriers—including one-way streets with no parking that function like freeways so that one block is cut off from the next, or you start putting in berms that supposedly protect one use from another but really just isolate them, or when you create housing pods that only connect to the rest of the world by one entrance to the housing development—then things do not seamlessly connect to each other.

—James Howard Kunstler, September 16, 2010
KunstlerCast #125: "Cassandra"

Mandating Suburbia

Duncan Crary: It's practically illegal to build a healthy urban organism in suburbia because of the zoning codes, which are almost identical everywhere. Even in a lot of cities, we now have zoning codes that prevent anyone from building *in the city* the way cities are supposed to be built—buildings that are close together, multiple stories high, with mixed uses and little or no parking. How did we end up doing things this way?

James Howard Kunstler: It's also a tortured story that goes back to the early twentieth century when the city was changing very rapidly, becoming an extremely unpleasant place. Again, the scale of industry was getting enormous—an automobile plant in the 1920s was huge!—and it was all mixed in with the other stuff. It was hurting property values.

So we developed this idea in the early twentieth century that you had to rigorously segregate all the uses in the city. The residential neighborhoods had to be rigorously cordoned off from the places where industry was allowed to do its thing and be dirty, and noisy, and smelly and all that. That became the classic model for zoning.

DC: One of my favorite stories from Troy, New York, involves a guy who got snubbed by the elitists and so he got revenge by building some horrible-smelling soap factory as close to their homes as he could.[5] Before the zoning codes, you could get away with that kind of stuff.

JHK: That's the point. How do you regulate the behavior of these industrial activities which are taking our cities and making them unpleasant in a way that we've never experienced before? Zoning is supposedly the rational response to a set of circumstances which at the time were pretty difficult.

It's after World War II that we really start to get going on the refinements of zoning, and we enter this territory of the absurd—especially in suburbia where all the construction is happening. Among the things we do is that we decide shopping is now classified as an obnoxious "industrial activity" that nobody should be allowed to live anywhere near.

Not only does that create huge problems for traffic—by doing that you mandate that everybody has to get in their car eleven times a day to make a trip for every little thing they need—but you've also now eliminated the most common kind of affordable housing that is found virtually everywhere else in the world, except the United States after 1950, which is: people living above retail establishments, above stores—normal urban typologies of buildings that are more than one-story high.

After 1950, we built very few commercial retail buildings that were more than one-story high. That engenders this unanticipated consequence of having an affordable housing crisis. We're now obliged to provide this artificial commodity called "affordable housing" because we were too stupid to provide it organically by allowing buildings to be more than one-story high.

DC: In *The Geography of Nowhere* you mentioned that a lot of towns across America adopted the same set of zoning codes.[6]

JHK: There was an engineering company that built a template for zoning for pretty much any municipality. It was like the generic vanilla zoning code.

DC: Which is why every housing development in America looks almost the same?

JHK: There was also a very firm consensus among the people who are delivering suburbia about how things should be done—the traffic engineers, the developers, the real estate salespeople all agree that this is the way we should do it. The streets should all be eighty feet wide. The houses should all be on a half-acre lot. The shopping centers should all be far away from this so that people aren't bothered by grocery shopping.

And that's how it becomes normal. The consensus is adopted by all the professional organizations, like the American Society of Highway Engineers and all of their cohorts, and the professional builders, etc. For about sixty years now we've had

this very firm agreement about how this stuff should all work. The fact that this is all on the verge of collapsing now is another story. But as one of my favorite correspondents never tires of saying, "Shit happens, and shit un-happens."

DC: And that's how, in your assessment, urban planning became all about following and enforcing these codes instead of actually making plans for good urbanism?[7]

JHK: Urban planning has no design component anymore. It's simply about administering the codes and about the minutiae and trivia of measuring the width of the curb cut—making sure that the signage is exactly within a centimeter of the specifications. It has nothing to do with excellence in design or having standards of excellence, or having a consensus for excellence, or least of all any consideration for how the buildings will behave in their relations with the other buildings so that we have some kind of a coherent urban structure. That's totally absent.

They threw it in the garbage in about 1950. They decided, "We don't need this anymore. All we need is the traffic engineering, and the highway geometries and statistical analysis. Nothing else is necessary. So here's five thousand years of architecture and urban design, and we're throwing it in the dumpster now along with the old Boston cream pies and the half-eaten tuna fish sandwiches."

DC: I'll never forget when one of the town planners in this big suburban mess of a place told me that he was looking forward to moving to Manhattan when he retired so that he could actually live in a walkable mixed-used community. This was a guy who'd been enforcing the zoning codes that didn't allow for mixed use in this town for decades.

JHK: Well these poor bozos, they come out of planning school—because they made some bad choice, or they were deceived into thinking that they were in a design discipline—and then they spend the next forty years just working for a pension plan. They hate their work. They hate themselves for doing it. They realize that the whole thing is a mummery. Finally they gaze at that golden, glowing finish line of retirement, when they can go to a place where it's exciting, that has mixed uses—a place that, in short, displays all the qualities that they've been preventing from occurring in the place they're in charge of for their whole career. The damage that these municipal officials have done all over America is just out of this world.

Main Street, USA, Disneyland

At the heart of Disneyland is Main Street, USA. This is the little town of Marceline, Missouri, that Walt Disney spent most of his childhood in. This is the recreation of his memory of what small-town America was like back when small-town America was still pretty good, in the period before the First World War.

What's so fascinating about it is that Americans come from all over America to walk in a Main Street environment that is not tyrannized by automobiles, where some attention has been paid to putting some pretty buildings up. To call them beautiful is taking it too far, maybe. By American vernacular standards, they employ conventions that we think of as being decorative. We call it Victorian, although God knows it's a hodgepodge of stylistic things.

But they come from their little towns in Michigan and Minnesota and Kansas and Arkansas and Georgia, and they flock to Disneyland to be in a Main Street environment that is spiritually rewarding. Then they go back to their little towns in all these places and destroy their own hometowns.

These are the same guys who sit on the zoning boards who make the decisions to turn their own Main Street into a six-laner, to knock down all the street trees, to make the sidewalks four inches wide. Then after they do that, they pack up the family and go back to Disneyland so they can feel good about America. This is so perverse.

—James Howard Kunstler, December 24, 2009
KunstlerCast #94: "The Disneyfication of America"

Reforming the Codes

DC: How do you feel about efforts to reform the zoning codes?

JHK: For twenty years, I've been watching the New Urbanists[8] go into locality after locality and fight these battles to reform the zoning codes and the planning laws and the regulations. I've been in the charrettes and the public meetings many times and watched it happen. It's often a heartbreaking process. Sometimes you go through two or three stages of these public meetings where you actually form a consensus with the various so-called stakeholders. Then it gets down to the city council actually voting on a new set of codes, and they don't do it. That happens time and time again. Either that or they actually hire some New Urbanist planner who really has the expertise to do this kind of thing, a guy like Joel Russell in Northampton or Victor Dover in Miami or Andrés Duany's company, DPZ.

They'll go in there and they'll actually meticulously write a whole new so-called "smart code," a term that I'm not all that happy with, because it tends to alienate that portion of the population that knows they're dumb—they tend to be the pro-sprawlers—so they don't like to hear somebody brandishing a "smart code" because it implies that there's another side that's not smart. But it was within the cultural trends of our locutions of the moment, when everything was "smart"-this and "smart"-that—smartphones, smart-etc. They've had quite a bit of success when you consider what they're up against.

But my own feeling is that rather than reform all of these codes, I think they're simply going to be ignored as we move into this more difficult future, this "Long Emergency" as I call it. I don't think we're going to have the mental energy, or even the administrative resources, to accomplish the reform of our zoning codes. I think that in the future people will just ignore them. It will be obvious that we can't require nine parking spaces for every commercial place that opens. Rather than legislatively try to change that in our city codes, we'll simply say, "Look, this is obviously ridiculous. Forget about it. Don't bother." Because we won't be driving as much. There will be fewer cars and less of a need to deal with it. That's what I see. So they'll be ignored, and then, after a passage of time, when we can kick back a little bit and we have a little bit of mental leisure recovering from these hardships and blows and discontinuities, we'll create a new set of norms and standards for how we do things.

Children of the Burbs

Duncan Crary: One of the first things I hear people say when they choose the suburbs over living in an urban place is, "I have children. I've got to raise children."

James Howard Kunstler: When people say that, generally what it means is that they're afraid to send their kids to schools in a city—and behind that are racial issues that are too toxic for Americans to have a public discussion about. But then there are the other aspects of living in suburbia for a child that go beyond school, that have to do with giving them a supposed "normal" life. But what happens is they end up having a pretty abnormal life in the burbs.

DC: Is raising children in suburbia good for them?

JHK: Raising children in the suburbs has a lot of drawbacks. Apart from the school issues, kids over seven years old have a tough time in the suburbs. Under seven, they don't really have to go anywhere. They're happy in their little cul-de-sac, playing cops and robbers or flies up. That was my experience the three years I lived in the suburbs between the age of five and eight. That was OK.

The trouble starts a little bit later when they have to become socialized. And by that I don't mean becoming socialists, I mean learning how to use their daily environment themselves and developing their own sense of sovereignty—that tends not to occur in the suburbs, because it's too hard for kids to get places. They can't get to their soccer match by themselves. They can't get to their clarinet lesson.

So the family "chauffeur," which is usually Mom, ends up taking them to all of these places. A kid doesn't develop any sense of moving through space under his or her own power.

Now I happen to live in a classic Main Street town that is set up so that kids really can get to things on their own. They do come to downtown Saratoga Springs, and they do go to the coffee shop. They go to the stores. They buy things. They learn how to do things that will eventually lead them into being fully functioning adults. Kids in the suburbs don't learn how to do that—Mommy does everything for them.

When I was a kid in 1957, my parents divorced and I moved from the suburbs of Long Island into Manhattan at the age of eight. Previously, my whole life was centered around throwing baseballs on the cul-de-sac and riding my little bike. Then I got into Manhattan, and I didn't even have a bike anymore—that was over with. My whole life, all of a sudden, was about learning how to get on a Madison Avenue bus, to go from point A to point B—learning how to take the cross-town bus from 86th Street to the planetarium at the Museum of Natural History.

That was kind of a scary thing for an eight-year-old to learn how to do, but I did it. Then I got over it and I wasn't scared anymore. I was just a normal person using the city.

DC: I grew up in the burbs. It was great until I hit this sort of dead zone between the age of like thirteen and sixteen, where you can't drive.

JHK: Yeah, and your needs at that point are greater than they were when you were seven years old. You need to be connected to stuff, and you're frustrated continually by not being able to do it.

DC: So you start doing drugs in the rumpus room in the basement and listening to gangsta rap instead.

JHK: Playing with Dad's guns.

DC: It's true. I suppose that behavior goes along with how we send our kids to suburban schools that look like penitentiaries.

JHK: I don't understand why the schools look so terrible and scary— why it's necessary to do that. Obviously we didn't do that in an earlier period. If you go up to Glens Falls, New York, there's the old high school, which was converted into apartments. It's a wonderful, dignified building. It fits in with the city. It sends a message that what goes on here is all about the eternal verities. The school building is a neoclassical building, so it sort of speaks in the language of the classical verities. Then you go see the new junior high school on Route 9 in Saratoga, it looks like an insecticide factory, as Tom Wolfe put it.[9]

DC: The public high school in the suburban town where I lived looked like that. But I went to private school in a city—the Albany Academy, which is a beautiful neoclassical building that *looks* like an institution of learning.

JHK: By saying this, I don't think that either one of us is necessarily pimping for neoclassicism as the only way to decorate a building, or the only way to design something. It happens to be an architectural language that's suited to our democratic society, our republic. It takes the idea from Greece of being a democracy, and the idea from Rome of being a republic, and combines them.

We express that in a lot of our civic buildings: schools, libraries, museums, courthouses. But there are plenty of other wonderful styles of architecture. It's not about style. It's about making a statement to the user of the building that this is a dignified place. That it's an honor to be here—a privileged activity goes on in here, it's not punishment. But with our mentality of just creating "facilities" rather than actual typological buildings like schools, churches, etc.... When everything is a facility, it's really nothing. A "facility" is also a prison. In fact, most of our prisons are now officially called "facilities."

We've gotten into a lot of trouble by sort of technologizing these things. And we manage to take all of the artistry and humanity out of them.

An Environment that Teaches Hyper-individualism

DC: There's something else about the suburban environment that seems to give children disturbing ideas about ownership and private property and the concept of sharing. When I was a kid in the burbs one of the most common disputes, at least, among the boys—when we got mad at each other, we would say, "Get off my property." We would have these arguments over property lines. Eight-, nine-, ten-year-old kids! Did you experience any of that when you were a kid out there?

JHK: It's funny that you mention it. I seem to dimly remember exactly those kinds of things. I guess what it shows is that the exaggerated sense of hyper-individualism out in the suburbs is even communicated to eight-year-old kids.

The Impoverishment of Public Places

DC: It's very hard as a teenager in the suburbs to find good public places where you can hang out with your friends and not get chased off for loitering. I remember hanging out in a storm sewer culvert with my teenage friends. That was our idea of a good spot.

JHK: The whole key to understanding the suburbs has to do with the impoverishment of the public places and the glorification of the private realm. We have more bathrooms per inhabitant in our houses than any other nation in the world, but we have extremely poor public places in most of suburban America, which is most of America. Most of the public places for kids are the leftover scraps—the berms, the parking lots, the places that nobody really cares about.

We have very few places that demand respectful behavior from the kids, and so you put them in a place like that and they are going to tend to be as wild as possible. You put them in a berm between the

Walmart and the K-Mart and they're going to torture kitty cats and make homemade tattoos and smoke bongs and drink aftershave. That's how they behave in the public place of the berm in suburbia.

You get incredible volumes of terrible behavior. And they're usually unsupervised. There are no adults around to regulate torturing the kitty cats and stuff like that. If there were sensitive adults around, that wouldn't happen. It ends up being an environment that does not prepare kids to be successful, caring adults.

DC: Teenagers in the burbs don't seem to have a lot of adults around. But the younger kids can't seem to get away from their parents—parents tend to micromanage their lives.

JHK: You know, one of the things that's so different about the way young children have been living in recent decades is that there's almost no unplanned casual time. What kids really need is unscripted roaming around their environment—beyond just the playgrounds that have been designed for them. They need to be around buildings and shopping and places where adults are doing things and where policemen are, and where ordinary citizens are doing their business, and where people are making things and doing things that are useful.

They also need to be able to cross the boundary from the urban environment into nature. That boundary was everywhere until about 1950. It was one of the great things about the way life was. There really were no big broad suburban areas, except in maybe London, England, or New York City, etc. But until then, in most small towns in the USA, you'd walk to the edge of town, and you were out of town. It's important for kids

to be able to make that journey and then go about their unplanned play and imaginative construction of their world.

DC: I was very active outside as a young kid growing up in the suburbs in the eighties. But the developments hadn't overtaken all of the old abandoned farm fields yet, so I still had access to the woods nearby. The kids growing up there today don't have as many places to run around in the wild. But you know, the parents today seem to be more afraid to let their young children out alone anyway....

JHK: When I was five or six, we moved out to a development in Roslyn, Long Island, that was right behind the remnants of an old derelict estate that belonged to a guy named Clarence Mackay, who was a telegraph magnate of some kind.[10] The mansion was abandoned and half ruined and the grounds had these marvelous carriage drives lined with azalea bushes and stuff. It was really quite grand.

My backyard ran right up against that, so we could ramble around in this three-hundred-acre estate. Then it underwent a very severe change. Another developer came in and plotted out a new addition to the suburban development that we were in and devastated the forest and brought in the bulldozers and created the new streets—all within a couple of years from the time that we moved in.

At the same time, there was a character on the loose named "The Mad Bomber." He was like one of the first great serial bombers of the modern age, at least the post-war age. His name was George Metesky—he was just some crank from Connecticut who was leaving bombs here and there. I don't even remember whether he actually killed someone. But he was some joker in a raincoat or something who terrorized the New York metropolitan area. I remember my friends and I saw a car parked on this carriage drive in the forsaken estate behind my house. And we got it in our heads that this was the Mad Bomber who was hanging out in this car.

The only reason I'm telling you this dumb story is because it has to do with walking to school. I went to a little grammar school about a half a mile from our suburban development, in one of the residue villages of the north shore of Long Island. It was called Greenvale. And it had been there a couple of hundred years. It had a little grid of streets. It had the pre–World War II houses, and it had a grammar school that had been built in the 1920s—a little red brick building. And we walked there from the suburban development, through quite an obstacle course of things.

First you left the development and crossed a major street. Then we went through a woody kind of wilderness that must have been about a four-acre woods—not yet developed into a supermarket, which it later became. Then we had to cross Route 25-A, which was a major four- or six-laner, even back then. Finally, from there, we went into the little grid of Greenvale, which was fairly safe—it had some sidewalks, etc. But we did this when we were five and six years old, going to the first grade!

DC: Yeah. Sure.

JHK: Nobody bothered to escort us or drive us to school. We were programmed fairly efficiently to find the place. We knew how to get there. We even knew how to find the path across the four-acre wilderness of woods to get to Route 25-A, Northern

Boulevard. We were five and six years old, going to Miss Schneider's class in the first grade of the Greenvale school. No problem. Nobody worried. And I don't know where we got this idea about the Mad Bomber, probably from our parents, because we didn't read *The New York Times*.

DC: They still let you go out, even though they knew the Mad Bomber was out there. I had a lot of unsupervised experiences like that, too—running around through the woods and riding my bike all over the place. I had a pretty good childhood in the burbs until those early teen years. But one of the lingering psychological effects I have from the experience is that I feel anxiety whenever I find a nice, open, "undeveloped," natural place. Because when I was growing up in suburbia the landscape got gobbled up so fast as I grew older. Now I don't want to get attached to any patch of woods or field or anything because I figure it'll just get destroyed eventually. Do you experience that kind of anxiety?

JHK: Oh yeah. Tony Hiss wrote a wonderful book back in the late eighties called *The Experience of Place* in which he said pretty much that nobody in America anymore feels that they are entitled to go back home and find it being the same thing that it was when they left a few years earlier.

The rate of change has been terrible. It's not just the rate of change. It's the quality of the changes that have taken place, because almost everything we've built in the last fifty years has made people uncomfortable or made their lives worse. In fact, that's what's really behind so much of the NIMBY activity today, when the demonstrators come out.

DC: "Not in my backyard" that stands for.

JHK: Right. First, the bulldozers show up. Guys in the yellow hard hats. And then the NIMBY protesters come out. They don't want anything new built next to them because all these things have made their lives worse. The old expression is they don't want a house just like their house next to their house.

DC: It's funny because the word "development" has been so hijacked that I've come to dread it. "Development" should be a positive word, shouldn't it?

JHK: Yeah. But to us it just means a new parking lot will appear next to your house.

DC: Would you go as far as to say that raising children in suburbia is a form of child abuse?

JHK: Well, I don't think it's that far off the mark. But I would hasten to say that we overdo the whole abuse angle a lot. We've become hysterical puritans in that sense in our time. But it may be a response to the fact that we are inflicting a lot of damage on ourselves and find that we can't stop doing it.

We can't stop inhabiting our suburban environments, because we've invested so much of our national wealth in them. They're there! The vast housing tracts, etc.—they're there. And they are indeed very punishing for the development of children, who require certain things growing up in a human habitat that they don't get in suburbia. But, obviously, this is mostly unintentional. Most people move to these places because that's what we've got in America. We don't have a whole lot of choice, especially when it comes to the schools.

People are making these decisions because they feel like they are compelled to make them. It's just unfortunate. The suburbs are not good places for kids. The cities are not really adequate either, the way most of them are in America.

You know, New York City has a lot of wonderful amenities and attractions and opportunities, but it's really an overwhelming place. I don't think that kids necessarily feel comfortable in it. The scale of the streets and the buildings is huge. The traffic is overwhelming and frightening. There are very few places in Manhattan or Brooklyn that are

The Family Room

The man's den went through a double transition. It mutated from being a male space to the place where the TV is watched. But now it's become something else again. It's become the place where all the plastic children's crap is strewn all over—the "family room," where you can't even walk without tripping over a three-foot-long plastic turtle. And so now, not only have the males had their space taken from them, but the adults generally have been banished from the family room. In many ways the word "family" in American lingo is a hidden synonym for "This is something for children."

—James Howard Kunstler, August 20, 2009
KunstlerCast #76: "Man Caves"

scaled well for kids, and that's one of the better environments in the US. You go outside of New York, and you start talking about Akron, Ohio, and Kansas City. It's really hard. For me, the default solution would be small-town America, but a lot of people don't have the ability to get there, and there isn't that much of small-town America left that's still OK. A lot of it is really struggling.

Around here, where we are, the town of Saratoga Springs is doing fairly OK. It's healthy. But most of the other towns around here are in a post–Soviet backwater haze of desolation and dereliction. Their school systems are suffering. Physically, the places are deteriorating.

It's a really tough one—where are you going to live in America? You can count on your hands the places that are really wonderful—there are very few places that are even adequate beyond that.

Sprawling to Obesity

Duncan Crary: The other day I was reading *Planning* magazine, which is published by the American Planning Association. There was a viewpoint piece at the end titled "We Knew It All Along."[11] It was about the link between the obesity rate and the suburbanization of America. Apparently the American Academy of Pediatrics estimates that 32 percent of American children are overweight due in large part to inactivity. And this group of pediatricians has gone on the record linking the child obesity rate in America to the way we've designed our built environ-

Land Whales

The most common species seen at a mall typically in the United States is the animal called the land whale, and we just saw several of them pass. The sidewalk was quaking under their tread.... They're headed off to graze at the fried food buffet.

—James Howard Kunstler, September 8, 2008
KunstlerCast #30: "Twilight of the Mall Era"
Recorded at Colonie Center, Albany, New York

ment to be so car-dependent…
in other words, so suburban. So the author of this op-ed piece in *Planning* magazine was essentially making the point that—Duh! We knew this all along as urban planners, but now we have medical proof that we can no longer afford to ignore this issue.

James Howard Kunstler: It is amazing that this comes from the professional magazine of the people who actually bring suburbia to you—or at least the officialdom that presides over its construction and design. Yeah, it's a big duh.

They're about forty years behind in admitting it and reporting it, though. Because the damage that's been done to a few generations of Americans now is out of sight. I just saw a statistic that the percentage of obese Americans now is much higher even than it was in 1990. So we're heading off the charts. It's also interesting that this coincides with this cultural and economic crackup that's underway. It couldn't happen at a worse time: the physical condition of our citizens is so bad at the very time when they probably need to be in much better shape just to succeed in life and be successful organisms under new rather stringent terms.

DC: Obesity has overtaken smoking as the number one cause of death in the US.

JHK: It's not surprising. The amazing thing is that we went through this half-century project of constructing the suburban living arrangement and we didn't notice what was going on—especially when you get into this transition between how children use their environment in a traditional human habitat, and the way that we've now started working around the fact that everything is disconnected.

DC: A lot of people in the US don't even walk for twenty minutes a day. That's scary.

JHK: You see a quite different way of life, especially for adults, in European cities. You go to Paris and people walk all over Paris. It's very well designed for that. They also have the cultural component of being used to not eating huge portions of things. You go into a restaurant and you get a reasonable amount of food on your plate.

In America, food is sort of an entertainment, so you're trying to stimulate people's frontal lobes the way you would with a movie. You go into a chain restaurant like Ruby Tuesday or Friday's—it's all about stimulating your brain visually and not really about nutrition, or even about good eating. So that's one of the side effects of being such an ultra entertainment-oriented society, that food is much more about tickling your brain cells than it is about nutrition.

But it's not just kids, it's everybody. I was trapped in a chain motel overnight at the Denver airport and there was only one place to eat within walking distance. It was a Ruby Tuesday chain restaurant. So I went there, and it was really startling. I just hadn't been in one of these places for years. It was full of people who were supersized human beings, all eating something that was twice as big as their head, with a side of French fries and dessert. After these people consumed these immense plates of nachos and blooming onions, or giant French fry concoctions, they would bring these barges of ice cream and chocolate and stuff.

It's just no wonder that Americans are so huge, and no doubt it's part of this massive infusion of corn products that we hear about that get into everything—meat, and crunchy things, and cookies, and chips, and virtually everything that is now part of the American diet. That's all happening because we're pouring oil on the croplands to produce all this stuff. So there's a whole chain of circumstances out there that are really pretty tragic.

DC: If I were to take this pediatrics study about obesity and the built environment to a suburban planning board to argue against another car-dependent development, what do you think the reaction would be?

JHK: Knowing what I know about the permitting and approvals process, I don't think that it would make much of an impression on them. There have been plenty of arguments, even before this one, that building suburbia was not a good idea. But that didn't affect anybody's project. So it's just another argument among many that have been used to try to break a set of very bad habits. The bad habits have been so profitable that they simply can't be overcome. I don't think they will be. I think that what will overcome them will be events that mandate changed behavior.

DC: Just to concede the counterargument here, it is possible to live a sedentary life in an urban environment. You don't have to walk everywhere in the city. You can ride the bus. You can take the subway. You can sit on your couch and just watch TV and surf the Internet. If you're a kid, there are certain city neighborhoods that aren't conducive to playing in. I mean it is still possible to become sedentary and obese even in a great urban neighborhood.

JHK: Sure. Especially if you're still living in a culture that's producing a lot of corn syrup, and sugary treats, and Rice Krispie bars and hamburgers. That certainly would play a huge role.

DC: And still driving everywhere.

You can still drive everywhere in cities—you almost need to in some of the smaller cities that don't have good transit. I live in a very urban neighborhood in a small city. But even people who live in this neighborhood will drive to get to other places in the same neighborhood that they could easily walk to.

JHK: The condition that these places are in now is also anomalous. It seems like they've been that way forever, and that they'll continue to be that way forever. But I don't think so. I think that we're heading for big changes fairly rapidly.

DC: I guess the trick is that we need to have an environment that you can walk through without paying attention to the fact that you're walking. In suburbia, if you walk anywhere, it's like you're solely going for a walk—

JHK: It's an ordeal.

DC: There's no other purpose to

walking in suburbia other than the activity of walking—unless you're walking the dog. There are no destinations to walk to.

JHK: This is precisely the difference between being in one of those really wonderful, old-world cities and being in the US. When you're in Europe, if you go to Paris for a week's vacation, you go out every day at eight o'clock in the morning, and by the time you get back to your hotel room at five, you've gone fourteen miles on foot. But you didn't notice it, because it was so interesting, because your mind was diverted for 90 percent of the time. There was something to catch your attention. There was something beautiful to look at, something interesting in a shop window, a beautiful street that you were on. It's just such a diverting and rewarding experience, you simply don't notice.

In the best places, that's how it is for the people who actually live there day in and day out. It's one of the reasons that when you go to Paris, you just don't see that many fat people on the street. Because walking around a place like that is tremendously rewarding and it makes you want to do it more.

The Architecture of Suburbia

Duncan Crary: Before we get into specifics, what can you say in general about the buildings that make up suburbia?

James Howard Kunstler: Most of them aren't really architecture—they're just manufactured boxes. They're depressing. They give us the

Where the Sidewalk Ends

In America we should change our national motto from "In God We Trust" to "It's The Thought That Counts," or "We Meant To." American life is so full of empty gestures and we see so many empty gestures in the built environment, including the sidewalks that end after sixty feet.

—James Howard Kunstler, June 12, 2008
KunstlerCast #18: "Pavement"

message that we don't care about ourselves or our surroundings. They give us the message that we're incompetent. And these are all unhealthy things to believe about yourself, especially collectively as a culture.

DC: What are the defining characteristics of the suburban home?

JHK: The whole idea of suburbia is that it started out being country living. It was the counterpoint to city life, which for many decades in America was considered a really unpleasant, undesirable thing, to get away from if you could possibly manage to do it. So the whole idea of the suburban house is that it's going to be a country house. But it goes through this mutation, especially after the Second World War, where the whole orientation of everyday life is no longer a counterpoint between the city and the country— it's simply a place in the service of the car. So increasingly, the suburban house becomes not a country house, but a cartoon of a country house in a cartoon of the country. It's especially interesting that this occurs just at the time in American history where we're becoming a cartoon society ourselves, where television is starting to impose its ethos on us and everything is becoming some kind of a televised image cartoon for us. So we naturally morph from a people who care about the way we build our things into people who just start using gestures and suggestions when we build things.

DC: There are shutters that don't actually function, for example.

JHK: They're stick-on appliqués on a box that might as well be a packing crate. Nothing functions. The porch doesn't function, unless you're a leprechaun and you're eighteen inches high—there's not enough room to put a chair on it. It's all a gesture.

For years we've been building these suburban ranch houses with picture windows, and the whole supposition was that you have a picture window so you can see the picture outside your window. But who wants to look outside the window in Levittown at a bunch of houses that look exactly like your house across a boring street full of Chevrolets? Nobody wants to do that. You end up having to put on window dressings and treatments to prevent you from not only looking out, but to prevent other people from looking in through this vast wall of glass to see you walking around in your pajamas at ten o'clock at night.

DC: In the newer suburban developments, I've been in houses that have these very large entrances. No one actually enters through the front door, though, because you enter through the garage. But the ceilings in the front entrances to these houses are incredibly tall. I like tall ceilings in old buildings. But that's not what we have here. It's not quality space. It's just big.

JHK: They're attempts to proclaim your status as a new kind of royalty. There are various names for them. Sometimes the builders in the Sunbelt call it "The North Dallas Special." The other name for this is the "lawyer foyer," which is supposed to be the impressive entrance of an upper-middle-class squire with a twenty-foot entrance and a gigantic Plexiglas chandelier that looks like a spacecraft hanging down. In suburbia you have more space in your house than even the kings of medieval Europe experienced.

DC: I've been to some medieval castles, and you're not exaggerating by that much.

JHK: People today are living in levels of opulence and luxury in terms of private space that are unheard of in the history of the human race.

Vinyl Siding

DC: Of course one of the symbols of suburbia is the vinyl siding on the outside of houses. Vinyl siding sucks, Jim, but I've been meaning to ask you: *why* does vinyl siding suck so much?

JHK: Well, I would attribute it partly to the diminishing returns of technology, a much overlooked and underappreciated phenomenon in our time. What that means is that you create some wonderful tool or device or manufactured substance, and it seems to be a wonder material. And you don't discover, until you've used it for a while, that it has all these weird side effects and unintended consequences that you never thought of. Like we've created this whole industry for vinyl siding. Fine. People call up the company: "I've got a house that's energy inefficient. We need to put this envelope around it of plastic stuff that looks like wooden clapboards, and wooden soffits—it's all going to be plastic now."

You go put it up, and within five years the ultraviolet light has started to attack the vinyl and made it look splotchy or started to warp it. And the soffits start to fall apart and hang off, and the window surrounds start to warp and tweak and twist. It looks terrible. It stops working the way it was designed to work, because now it leaks again. We just sell ourselves a bill of goods that some technological wonderful wonder material is going to solve all our problems.

There's another thing to it, too, that we don't take into account. This actually started earlier with the aluminum siding people and all that crap—the pressed stone and all the applied surface stuff. The salesmen would come around and they would tell you, "Here's this wonderful stuff. It's virtually no maintenance." In the old days it was assumed that you had to maintain the exterior of your house. This is just part of the human condition. But now you have the salesman telling people, "Oh, it's no longer part of the human condition. You don't have to take care of your house."

Now we have these houses all over America that have been acquiring a patina of auto emissions for decades. You start to see this gray soot accumulating under the eaves and at the edges and on the porch roof. The house gets dingier and dingier. But the guys who own it won't clean it, because they were told as part of the contract for sale that "It's no-maintenance—you never have to do anything to it." So even though they see that it's starting to look crappy and grubby, "By golly, I'm not going to maintain it!" And that's one of the reasons that the houses covered with these materials look so crappy.

DC: Even when the stuff's brand new I don't like it. To me it's just not real.

JHK: Well it isn't real. It's pretending to be something else.

DC: Why do I care that it's not real? Why does that bug me so much?

JHK: I think that we are disturbed by the inauthentic. Vinyl siding pretends to be wood, and we know it's not wood, and it pisses us off that we're being lied to by a physical object. A lot of these plastic cladding materials for buildings, especially the ones that try to pretend that they're wooden clapboards—they have wood grain embossed on them. The funny thing is, on real wood you almost never see the grain because it's been planed and sanded off, and when it's painted it doesn't really show. So the way that you know that

the siding is phony is if you see the wood grain. So why do they even bother? It looks terrible.

A Tremendous Hunger for Meaning

DC: There's a shopping outlet mall in Lee, Massachusetts, that I call "The Vinyl Acropolis." It's an entirely faux New England village on the Mass Pike. The Reebok shoe store might be in a building that looks like a church with a steeple. The Eddie Bauer store looks like it's the butcher shop or a barbershop. There's a brick-veneer clock tower in the middle of the parking lot. That kind of inauthenticity is really disturbing. But what's going on there with the architecture?

JHK: One thing it tells us is that people have a tremendous hunger for meaning in the things that they build, but they're not being delivered in a way that has any dignity. So what you end up with is an undignified and inauthentic artifact that just degrades people further.

DC: Are the people of the future going to be living in houses shaped like Pizza Huts, trying to reconnect with their culture the way nineteenth-century people were building houses that looked like Greek temples?

JHK: I doubt it. It's hard to predict what the nostalgic quality of that stuff will be, the little of it that survives. The nostalgia that we know now for that kind of thing has some particular names: "kitsch" is one of them. "Camp" is another term associated with that behavior. What that's about, really, is celebrating stuff for its vulgarity and awfulness. We consciously decide that it's wonderful because it's so bad—it's so pathetic, it's so bathetic that we celebrate the bathos in it. That kind of irony is only possible when you're living in a really luxurious culture, which is what the cheap energy culture has been. That provides us with the luxury to be ironic about this kind of stuff.

But the main feeling that's going to separate us in the future from what we've been doing in the past is: this shit's not going to be funny anymore. I think we're going to have the same attitude to Burger King and Pizza Hut that the people in Germany now have toward the Nazi regime. It's going to be something that we're ashamed of. It's going to be something that's going to be a deep, dark, forbidding, awful memory about the bad choices we made historically.

DC: Another thing that faux New England village outlet mall might show us is how we still have a vague hunger for regional differences in our architecture. Because we've lost any true regional differences in architecture out in the suburbs, haven't we?

JHK: Sure. One of the historical reasons you could tell the difference between being in a New England town and being in a tidewater Virginia town in the mid-Atlantic is because, down there, their vocabulary was brick and they developed a certain set of principles for ornamenting that—putting a certain kind of trim on it that was either black or white, and much of it was made along neoclassical motifs. In New England you got, basically, neoclassical wooden architecture. And in a way, that's a whole world of skill and methodology that's been more or less lost, but was recorded in things like Asher Benjamin's *The American Builder's Companion* book of the early nineteenth century.

Temples of Acquisition

DC: Do you ever shop in the mall?

JHK: There's a small mall in Saratoga near me, and I have to go there to get office supplies. That's about it.

DC: I try to avoid the place but sooner or later there'll be something I just gotta go there for. I always feel embarrassed when I'm at the mall, like I don't want to get caught there by someone who knows me. Do you feel embarrassed when you have to do that?

JHK: Oh, I don't feel embarrassed about it. For me it's just a mildly depressing experience to see where we've come after about thirty-five, forty years of this kind of behavior—to see it now at the dead end. A lot of the malls are full of all kinds of marginal business now, like wig shops, and stores that sell outfits for motorcycle thugs, and semi-pornographic gift stores. The cycle with these places when they enter their phase of dereliction is that all kinds of marginal activities move in.

DC: One of the things I always notice when I'm in a mall is how much the interior tries to look like a city street. There's tile instead of pavement, but basically what people are walking on in the center of the mall is the street. Some stores have facades like normal city buildings facing the "street." There are even trees growing in the middle of the mall.

JHK: None of these things are particularly surprising or unusual. Because whether you're on a real street or in a mall, you're dealing with a corridor of some kind and the best streets, of course, feel like comfortable corridors. The best streets in Europe, for example, are fairly intimate. There's nothing particularly wrong with that.

The problem with the mall is that it's disconnected from all the other activities of life besides shopping. It's disconnected from the places where people work, unless you work at the mall in retail. It's disconnected completely from the places where people live. For the most part, even the retail there is not necessarily everyday retail. You wouldn't go there to get a loaf of bread or the day's supplies for daily life or hardware. It's all dedicated to what we've come to call the consumer recreational shopping experience.

Abolish the Word "Consumer"

JHK: And let me revisit, for a moment, my campaign to abolish the word "consumer" from our discussions about these things. It's a very un-useful, demeaning, degrading term, because consumers have no obligations or duties or responsibilities to anything other than their desire to eat Cheez Doodles and drink Pepsi-Cola.

We need to call ourselves something else. Maybe "citizens" or something other than consumers. It's a very bad word. Because it also suggests that remaining a consumer society is a desirable end. And I think that has caused a huge amount of mischief.

One of the tragic things going on right now is that the consumer era is over. America is so unbelievably over-retailed. We don't need a single extra silver souvenir spoon shop in this country. Americans don't need any more *stuff*. They have too much stuff. And what we're going to be seeing in the months and years ahead is less activity both on the part of the customers, who we call "consumers," and the businesses that sell stuff to them. It's going to be fading into the background of our lives now. Capital is leaving the system and vanishing into a black hole as we discover that the American economy can't really run on an endless cycle of debt. So these huge temples of acquisition are now completely obsolete. This is really the end of the mall era. We're in the twilight of the mall era.

Retrofitting Malls and Box Stores

DC: In *Home from Nowhere* you discussed retrofitting malls. What do you think about these projects now, to break up the main building into smaller parts and integrate living quarters and things like that? Turning them into "Lifestyle Centers" and such?

JHK: In some places we've demonstrated that you can take a dead mall and infill the parking lots and create streets and deck over the one-story buildings. The thing is, most of that was done in the late twentieth century when we still had a lot of capital to invest in this nation.

We're in a new situation now. Capital is leaving the party. And we're going to have a lot less money to invest in anything, including the malls. What we're going to be doing is going back to the existing towns that were originally built before the Second World War that are really suited to the pedestrian experience—that's where the action is going to be.

DC: And how about the retrofit of all the box stores out there?

JHK: A lot of people have fantasies that they're going to be reused and turned into dance museums, and chiropractic hospitals and evangelical roller rinks. But my guess is most of them will be disassembled for their materials, for the salvage. All of these things will have value. As we get into more trouble with energy and finance, we're going to be hard up for

Country Living

The whole country living deal is kind of a fantasy that does not necessarily work out the way people imagine. The truth is people are social, they want to be around other people, they want to get together with their friends once in a while. In the best of all possible urban worlds you see your friends maybe once a day—not once a season when someone throws a party for spring—and that doesn't happen unless you're in some kind of coherent urban organism.

—James Howard Kunstler, June 30, 2011
KunstlerCast #162: "Triumph of the City"

a lot of building materials, especially stuff like steel I beams and aluminum trusses. So they'll have a lot of value for salvage. But eventually what you're going to see there are empty parking lots with weeds growing in them.

Picturing Suburbia

Duncan Crary: People might be surprised to learn that you spend a lot of time creating paintings of parking lots and McDonald's and Mobil stations.

James Howard Kunstler: I've painted my whole life. I went to a special school in New York City called the High School of Music and Art where we received a fair amount of decent training. It's something I've carried on in the background of my life forever. I'm what's called a *sur le motif* painter. I go out to the motif with my French easel and I'm out there with the subject matter in the field. I'm interested in the landscape of our time, and the landscape of our time is mostly about the highway.

Van Gogh painted the peasants sleeping next to the haystacks because he was in a landscape that was populated with human beings. I'm in a landscape that's populated mostly by automobiles, so I paint them. Edward Hopper did something similar. Although we look at Hopper's paintings today—his paintings from the 1920s and the '30s when he was doing a lot of his highway stuff—and we recognize that as a landscape that is now bygone because the scale of it is smaller and it all seems kind of quaint. It's not as overwhelming as what we've got.

Today it's very hard to see what you're looking at out there on a commercial highway strip, with all the contesting signage and all the visual clutter. So it becomes a great challenge to be able to make it legible. That's one of the things that I like about painting the highway strip.

I'm also interested in the contrast between the natural light and the artificial light, especially at sundown. I'll set my easel up in the juniper shrub bed of the Burger King to paint the K-Mart a quarter of a mile away, with the sun going down in a certain way so that the lovely kind of violet and purple and pink and orange and salmon-colored clouds will be contrasted to the bright primary colors of the electric signage. Sometimes it's beautiful, although it shouldn't be construed as a reason to promote suburban sprawl. It's out there. It's what we're living in. It's not going to be there the way it is now in fifty years. People will look back on these paintings, if they survive, and will see a landscape that looks different from what they're living in.

DC: When I first heard that you were painting these scenes, I assumed your paintings were going to be sarcastic. But they're not.

JHK: No, they're not ironic at all. I'm not trying to make a joke about it. I'm literally trying to be a straightforward reporter of the landscape of our time and its many moods.

I do like to paint in the evening. I found one particular strip mall nearby where the supermarket had a particular lighting scheme under the soffit. It allowed me to see the colors of my palette and the canvas very clearly while the rest of the stuff around was sort of dark. You could paint the McDonald's in the dark and still see what you're doing. That was a great boon to me.

I also found a lot of satisfaction in the industrial ruins that are all over this area of the Upper Hudson Valley. In fact, in the time that I've lived here over the last thirty years, a lot of the factories have been bulldozed, so that I was able to actually witness the process of demolition.

DC: I just bought an excellent book called *Hudson Valley Ruins* that goes up and down the Hudson Valley giving you the history of all of these ruins—many of them are industrial. There's one little nugget in the book that I especially like. The artists who belonged to the Hudson River School of Painters, America's first formal "school" of painting, were lamenting in their day that they didn't have any ruins in this country to paint.[12]

JHK: Absolutely, and the figures in that period—Thomas Cole, Albert Bierstadt, Frederic Church—would go through this initiation rite of traveling all the way to Italy to paint the ruins there as young men. They'd stay for a year or two or three and they'd make their bones by painting the ruins of Rome. Then they'd come back to America, and what they finally settled on was the idea that, "OK, we don't have ruins here, but we do have this wonderful romantic natural landscape. Let's make that our subject matter." So that became the subject matter of nineteenth-century American landscape painting, in the absence of having ruins. It became a kind of fetish.

The situation is different today. We have a lot of ruins out there. And when I go out, I feel very privileged, like Thomas Cole might have felt on the Roman Campagna, painting the disintegrating aqueducts of the Roman Empire. I go out to Clarks Mills by the Hudson River and I paint the ruins of the wallpaper factory there. It's sort of thrilling. It's also a thrilling place to be physically because it's a place of nebulous ownership. The Georgia–Pacific company actually owns the site but there's nobody there guarding it anymore. They've given up. The fences have big holes in them now so you can get in there. It's become a kind of a strange natural park that has no supervision.

So it's thrilling to be out there alone with an easel by the river. It's starting to get populated, too. There are people who are going through the fence and fishing along the river. Finally there are some human figures out there.

DC: Speaking of Thomas Cole, one of the painting series you referenced in *The Geography of Nowhere* is "The Course of Empire."[13] How did it influence you?

JHK: I certainly appreciate it, although I haven't done anything remotely like it.

Thomas Cole, the great American landscape painter, was interested in painting series of things. "The Course of Empire" depicts the rise and fall of the Roman Empire in five panels, although it's never stated, from the pastoral phase to the big buildings going up. Finally the climax is this huge pageant that's going on in this gigantic kind of amphitheater on the water. It's like a harbor but there seems to be some great spectacle of empire going on. Somebody has just returned from a remote land with giraffes and elephants and all this stuff. Then we get a little further and there's nobody there anymore and the buildings are disintegrating. Some kind of war has taken place. It's left a lot of damage. Finally we see the utter desolation of the ruins hundreds of years later. It's quite a tour de force of paintings.

DC: The funny thing is that if I were to come up with a more recent example of the same thing, I would think of Robert Crumb's "A Short History of America." Do you know that cartoon series?

JHK: Oh, it's fabulous—showing the development of a little country road into a small town, then into the beginning of the automobile age. All of a sudden the small town starts to fall apart. Finally it ends up in the 1980s as a convenience store, surrounded by all this crap of technology: the horrible broken signage and the telephone poles and the condensers and the electric installations and the trucks and just all the crap out there.

DC: Do you think Crumb was being ironic?

JHK: Oh, absolutely not, in the sense that it seemed to be remarkably straightforward reportage of what was going on. In fact, in that movie with Crumb[14] they show him drawing that kind of scene and he's sitting there saying, "You can't make this stuff up. You have to really pay attention to the details."

DC: At one point in the film, he says how once you start paying attention to transformers in the air and all the wires it just takes over—that's all you can focus on. That happened to me for months as soon as I heard him say that in the film, that was all I could pay attention to—how ugly it is. There's so much up there that you just ignore.

JHK: There is! When I'm out there painting that stuff, I edit some of it out. But I leave a lot of it in. If you tried to put it all in, two things would happen; it would become as visually illegible as it actually is, and you would drive yourself crazy.

DC: I was excited to see that you're quoted in *The R. Crumb Handbook*, right after "A Short History of America."[15]

JHK: Yeah, I didn't even know that until you showed it to me. But I'm very honored to be in R. Crumb's book because he's a great genius of our time.

DC: Right next to your quote there's a picture of this guy sitting on a milk crate in this dumpy abandoned yard and he says, "I just sort of went with the flow, man." It's perfect.

JHK: I know. Crumb's really got our number.

DC: So Jim, wasn't there some incident involving you painting at a Burger King?

JHK: Yeah, I was doing one of my paintings at a Burger King and the manager guy—this young man with a 23-hair mustache—came out and said, "That ain't allowed here!" And I wanted to mess with him a little bit so I said, "What? What ain't?" And he said, "That there!" I said, "What?" He said, "You know! What you're doing there!" I said, "Painting's not allowed, huh?"

We went through this for a while and I thought the situation was so ridiculous that I really wanted to have fun with him so I finally said, "Look. It's fine with me if you go call the sheriff and he can arrest me for painting at Burger King on their property. I'm sure that'll be great public relations for your company. Because I'll make sure that lots of people know about it. And it'll be real cool."

DC: Do you know if that actually did happen, it'd probably make the Associated Press wire?

JHK: Oh, absolutely.

DC: And you'd probably sell that painting for three hundred grand.

JHK: Yeah. I should have encouraged him. I should have actually been more provocative because then I would have made more money on the painting.

Sprawl Defenders

Duncan Crary: There are people out there who actually defend sprawl. What kind of arguments are they making?

James Howard Kunstler: They have a number of arguments, and they all seem specious to me.

DC: So what are the three main pillars of the pro-sprawl argument?

JHK: As I understand it, one pillar is the idea that sprawl is fine because people like it.

That was the premise of a book about sprawl by Robert Bruegmann, a professor at the University of Illinois, Chicago campus.[16] Basically his premise was sprawl is fine because people choose it, therefore it must be the best thing that we've got.

It's a circular argument, and it's silly. We did what we did because we could do it. At this certain point in history following the Second World War we had a huge amount of our own oil. We had a lot of cheap land outside of our cities, because this is a big nation geographically. We had a huge income stream from selling our manufactured goods to the nations we defeated in the war. So we were all set up for this, and we were predisposed by this idea that runs through American cultural history that city life ain't no good and that the way to

Private Property

There's a relatively new idea in America that Americans have a tradition of being able to do whatever they want with their land, and that any impediments placed against that are somehow un-American. This is a fallacy. It's really been the result of a propaganda campaign from the promoters of suburban sprawl and the real-estate industry who have been fighting against any kind of regulation. We actually have a long history and a fat body of law for land use and the regulation of things you can do on it and with it. There is a whole corpus of responsibilities, obligations and duties that come with land ownership that simply can't be ignored. And this all falls under the law—we can indeed tell people what to do with their land.

—James Howard Kunstler, December 4, 2008
KunstlerCast #41: "Private Property"

go is country living for everybody. We liked the idea of country life—it was consistent with the mythology of our national experience in settling the wilderness and fighting bears and bison and saber-toothed tigers. So that in itself was a very strong motivation for people doing what they did, even though it only has relative reality to it.

The bottom line is that, yeah, it was a choice. But sometimes cultures collectively make tragic choices, and we've carried the suburban thing too far. We elaborated it too much, and we ran ourselves up a cul-de-sac in a cement SUV without a fill-up. Now we're stuck with all this stuff built in the wrong place in the wrong way, and it's going to be a huge liability for us.

The second big theme with the pro-sprawl lobby is the idea that sprawl represents liberty—that the suburban mode of living happens because we live in a free country, and it represents the American spirit of liberty to do what you want to do with your land. We're all free individuals and that's wonderful.

What they overlook, of course, is that sprawl is mandated rigorously by government regulation at all levels, which counts every single parking space per square foot of retail, and rigorously defines how far apart the houses have to be, and what the setbacks are, and the square footage of the house, etc. So this idea that the suburban life is free from government regulation is a lie.

Suburbia is also subsidized by government, by the way. Huge wads of free government money are given to build the infrastructure for suburbia—to lay the sewer lines and the water lines, and build the highways and widen the roads.

DC: A lot of the mortgages are subsidized, and have been in the past. Now even the values of the houses in suburbia are benefiting from government intervention.

JHK: Then there's another final argument, which is the econometric argument, where they haul out these reams of statistics to show how "efficient" suburbia is. I had a father-in-law, a marriage or so ago, who was a scientist for IBM. His favorite book was *How to Lie With Statistics*.[17] That's what econometrics is all about. Economics is getting to be a line of work that's totally discredited.

The experience of any informed

citizen just reading the news in the last several years is a history of seeing how you're being gamed by economists using statistics to prove things that aren't true—to prove that the banks are solvent, to prove that the housing market is fine, to prove that the US government is not broke, to prove that we can keep dispensing Medicaid forever, and lots of other things. So I regard the econometric arguments as being full of falsehood and trickery, and having very little validity.

DC: How are the sprawl defenders trying to argue through econometrics that suburbia is efficient?

JHK: One of the ways they do it is to attack public transit, and to try to demonstrate that car dependency is, in fact, the best thing that we can do in our culture. Randal O'Toole has made a kind of second career of campaigning against public transit, and in particular against restoring railroad service. He's in favor of building more highways, and widening highways, and doing everything we can to increase motoring volumes. Most of the pro-sprawl econometric arguments are based on the whole highway and driving equation.

DC: Folks like O'Toole think public transit is inefficient because we have to subsidize it?

JHK: Exactly.

DC: It's unbelievable. President Obama just dropped hundreds of billions of dollars to repair our highway system. But you try to do a fraction of that for public transit and it's evil socialism. There's so much public space in America dedicated to the use and storage of cars, which are private property.

JHK: Right, and I'll use a little econometric myself: it's estimated that the average cost of supplying a parking space anywhere is about $8,000. Either the real estate company that owns the strip mall is going to pay for it, or the government's going to pay for it, or some combination. It's hugely expensive, not to mention the cost of building highways. And compared to railroads—or even light rail or any other form of public transit—it's a joke.

At the same time, we have to understand that a lot of these guys defending suburbia are paid shills for the sprawl-building industry.[18] It's not as though they're just selfless, misguided citizens. They're essentially rogues who are in the service of evil enterprises.

DC: How come you don't often debate these pro-sprawl figures in public?[19]

JHK: Well there are only a few of these guys out there who are shameless enough to get up and take these idiotic positions, maybe because they can't make a living any other way. I really don't know.

There aren't that many of these guys out there. There's Randal O'Toole and there's Robert Bruegmann. They're the two main guys. Then of course there's Joel Kotkin,[20] who was featured in a David Brooks' column in *The New York Times*, which had the incredible headline "Relax, We'll Be Fine."[21] The whole idea of Brooks' op-ed piece was that we don't have a problem with our economy. We don't have a problem with the American population. We don't have a problem with housing. We don't have a problem with suburbia. We're just going to stick everybody in suburbs, and they'll be fine. The suburbs will be retooled and improved and made even better than they are now. And we'll all just keep on driving around. No problem.

David Brooks is probably the most fatuous opinion writer that *The New York Times* has. He's the guy who wrote *Bobos in Paradise*,[22] about the Bohemian, yuppie generation settling into suburbia, and about how wonderful that was. David Brooks himself has been a champion of suburbia with no awareness at all of its shortcomings or its destiny. These are the kinds of people who are leaders in the media. So when I say that we have a comprehensive failure of leadership in America, I don't mean just politically. I mean we have a failure of leadership in business, the media, academia and in the profession of economics—everywhere. We're not doing too well in terms of understanding where history is taking us.

DC: What are small cities supposed to do when confronted with these pro-sprawl arguments and this pressure to suburbanize their habitat?

JHK: At this point, I don't really think we have to worry too much. Because it's becoming self-evident—and it will be more obvious every week—that we can't support this suburban lifestyle. That, in many ways, it's simply failing. People can't pay their mortgages. People can't commute long distances to jobs, if they're lucky enough to have them. The schools cannot continue to operate in the way that they have been. The gradual impoverishment of the suburban governments is going to be another enormous problem. So I think that the trends will reveal themselves and it won't require a strenuous battle to go out and argue with these pro-suburbia guys.

DC: Is it even worth arguing about? I constantly find myself getting riled up and arguing with people about suburbia. I'm not a politician. I'm not in any position of authority. Why the hell am I even arguing with people about the suburbs? Should I just laugh and live my life and stay out of it?

JHK: Well it's kind of sad and annoying to see people, especially your relatives, clinging to ideas that are just going to get them into trouble. Right now we have a public that is full of delusional ideas that are not helping us get through this period of hardship and difficulty that we face. Personally I think the most important thing that we have to do in this country is form a coherent consensus for action so that we can take ourselves into the future.

DC: So you think it is worthwhile to have these discussions and mini debates with people then?

JHK: I think it's tremendously frustrating, and usually feels like an exercise in futility. It's very discouraging, and sometimes you're tempted to lose your temper, or just get so emotional that you can barely articulate or even state your position clearly. And at the same time, you know that they don't even care. They're tuned out. They don't even want to hear it. So it's a hard thing to do.

But a public consensus is an odd creature. I think the way this finally resolves is in the way that the philosopher Schopenhauer stated—that new ideas are first ridiculed, then violently opposed, and then they're accepted as self-evident.[23] We're seeing that now.

Let's not forget the huge factor of the practical investments that Americans have in that way of life.

They've got their suburban house, which for many households represents the place where most of their wealth is imagined to be stored. Even if the value of the house is going down, they've put most of their savings into it. So people can't conceive of letting go of that. It's terribly difficult for them to entertain any idea that even remotely threatens that.

Then, secondarily, there are all the investments that we've made in the infrastructures for daily life in suburbia, including the schools and the roads and the municipal tennis courts and everything else—we don't want to lose those investments. We're also afraid because we have no real legacy of affection for urban places in America. We don't want to move back into Ralph Kramden's apartment in *The Honeymooners*. And it's true that suburban houses really are pretty luxurious compared to what you get in the city. If you read the real estate ads in *The New York Times*, for example, or in *The New York Observer*, you see that a four-bedroom Manhattan apartment with two or three bathrooms and a fireplace goes for eleven million dollars. You don't even get a basement with that. But in suburbia you can have the same darn thing for $500,000. People naturally view their private space as being very important.

What you get in New York City these days is a pretty small living space and storage space, but you have access to all the marvels and wonders and amenities of being in this great cosmopolitan city. The same is true, of course, in Paris or London or Rio de Janeiro or really any great metropolitan place.

The Politics of Place

Duncan Crary: I want to try to sort out the politics of place with you. What I want to know is if suburbia is a conservative place and if cities are liberal places. I'm very confused by political allegiances in America right now. And I think you summed up what's confusing me, back in 1995, when you were writing for *The Planning Commissioner's Journal.*[24]

James Howard Kunstler: Doesn't everybody get that magazine?

DC: I only found the article after clicking through links on various blogs. Here's what you wrote:

Places Not Worth Defending

We have about, you know, 38,000 places that are not worth caring about in the United States today. When we have enough of them, we're gonna have a nation that's not worth defending. And I want you to think about that when you think about those young men and women who are over in places like Iraq, spilling their blood in the sand. And ask yourself what is their last thought of home? I hope it's not the curb cut between the Chuck E. Cheese and the Target store! Because that's not good enough for Americans to be spilling their blood for. We need better places in this country.

—James Howard Kunstler, TED 2004
Filmed February 2004, Ted.com

The town where I live, Saratoga Springs, New York, like practically every other town in America, is under assault by forces that want to turn it into another version of Paramus, New Jersey, with all the highway crud, chain store servitude, and loss of community that pattern of development entails.

Ironically, the forces who are ready to permit the most radical damage to the town's historic character consider themselves the most conservative; while the groups most concerned with preserving the town's best features, and even enhancing them, have been branded radical.

JHK: Yeah, this was quite an inversion of the assumed roles. It was weird, because the Republicans in a small-town setting like the one I live in had become very much allied with—or they were just part and parcel of—the whole community of builders and bankers, and the highway guys, and the development people. And it became quite a force.

Also, because financing was so cheap and our technology had reached a certain point, you could make pretty severe changes in a town very quickly just by following the mandates of conventional zoning laws.

In our case here in town, we replaced some great historic fabric with a bunch of shitty 1950s suburban crap. We tore down the Grand Union Hotel—a huge building—in 1954 and put a strip mall on the site in the middle of the city with parking all around it. That was before my time here. But in my time, the same stuff was going on. We built another strip mall a block away from that in 1982 or something. So you saw this happening time and time again. And yet, these were the people who claimed to be conservatives. What were they conserving? They weren't conserving anything. They were destroying stuff.

And the people who were trying to defend the old existing character of the town, they were branded as radicals, communists—people who wanted to turn the social order upside down. Because the people in charge of the social order had become agents of destruction. So it was a very strange thing. But it was interesting that these agents of destruction, who were generally Republicans around here, were able to brainwash the voting public into believing that they were, in fact, the pillars of the community. They were really just a bunch of opportunists who went to rip off whatever opportunity they could.

DC: I don't think that's uncommon throughout the entire country.

JHK: No, it's the template for how things worked all over America for fifty years. It's just been worse in some places than others.

DC: What exactly do these "conservatives" think they're conserving?

JHK: Really, the only thing that they are conserving are their business practices, which enable them to make lots of money and to be the high-status people in their community, the people who make the rules and the decisions. I don't want to get into a whole kind of academic, politically correct power rant about the oppressors and the victims, because I don't quite see it that way. But it is really a matter of the leaders in a given culture developing a consensus about what's OK and having that lead to a pretty undesirable outcome.

DC: I can see why business leaders

would adopt this brand of politics in suburbia. But why do the individual residents?

JHK: As far as I can tell, the big deal about suburbia politically is that the people who live there have so much of their own personal wealth tied up in the value of the real estate that they own, that the defense of the value of that house becomes the overwhelming political preoccupation—whether it's reflected in the kind of school that your kid is able to go to, or just the money value of the building itself that you bought. So many of the struggles of suburbia boil down to the preservation of the monetary value of your house.

DC: I find it interesting that people often assume that I'm a liberal because I'm interested in urban planning, or environmental conservation or historic preservation. But I don't know what's actually that liberal about those things. I tend to think of myself as more of a traditionalist. I kind of feel like, "I'm a conservative," and the people calling themselves conservatives are using the term wrong.

JHK: We've got a lot of sorting out to do about these things, and they're not going to come out of the wringer the same way that they went in. In fact, we may not even use these kinds of terms anymore to describe the new situation that we find ourselves in.

DC: Which is?

JHK: We are facing the wholesale disintegration of the suburban arrangement. It doesn't have a long horizon. It's in trouble. Anybody with a little bit of sensitivity can pick that up already and sense it. And it has made people desperate.

I think the threats that these people feel, at perhaps some subconscious level, may make them very frightened, deep down, and insecure. I think that fear and insecurity is getting so extreme that it's leading to some really crazy political beliefs. And it accounts for a whole lot of the anger that's out there and for the anger that's expressed by people like Rush Limbaugh and Glenn Beck, who—to my mind, what they really stand for is the fact that the America of 1963 doesn't exist anymore. Maybe it was the America of their childhood when Rush and little Glenn were fourteen years old, and it's all gone. They're desperate to either reinstate conditions that are lost, or to save every fragment of anything that's still around.

DC: But your own views are a little nostalgic for the way life was before suburbia, aren't they?

JHK: The word "nostalgia" itself is interesting because it literally means homesickness. It became evident to me that part of the whole suburban dilemma is that as a culture, as a nation, as a people, we are tremendously homesick—not just for a box that we call "a home," but for a real dwelling place for our society that is worth caring about.

The chief characteristic of just about everything we built in suburbia is that it ended up being stuff that wasn't worth caring about. And that had tremendous cultural implications for us.

DC: What are *your* political beliefs, Jim? You have referred to yourself as a being a dissatisfied registered Democrat.

JHK: Yeah I'm sort of a mainstream sixties Democrat.

DC: What does that mean?

JHK: It means I believe in social justice and equality. It means I am not in favor of starting wars frivolously. It means that I have a healthy respect for the depredations of big business and big money. I suppose that's broad enough.

DC: I would think you are also a conservative in a way—not in the way the term has recently come to be defined—but you are a conservative as far as resources go and…?

JHK: I'd say I'm a conservative in the sense that I'm an anti-avant-gardist.

DC: What does that mean?

JHK: I don't truck with the cutting edge of my culture. I think that they're mostly a fallacious cutting edge and that they're not really taking us anywhere. The cutting edge of architecture and art, I think, is largely nonsense in our time. So yeah, I'm very conservative in that sense.

Boomers: Back to the Burbs

Duncan Crary: I want to talk with you about your generation, the Baby Boomers. You're thirty years older than me. You're sixty-two and I'm thirty-two. So you got a firsthand look at the 1960s scene.

James Howard Kunstler: I went to college during the absolute heart of the Age of Aquarius. I got there in 1966. I was on the five-year plan for various reasons, so I graduated in 1971 after a protracted senior year, which I did over again. And I sort of saw it all.

DC: Can you explain to me how your generation went from the hippie-nature-peace-love thing to doing the yuppie-Saab-driving-suburban-stockbroker thing?

JHK: Yeah. It's kind of unfortunate. The really best pieces of the Aquarian revolution were the back-to-the

So-Called Free Thought

The thing that astonishes me the most about my generation is how this generation that espoused free thinking and free inquiry and freedom of everything ended up becoming the thought police.

And they ended up being the people at Harvard and Yale who said, "Well, we believe in diversity and multiculturalism as long as your diversity and multiculturalism is just like ours. And if you have a different version of the world, we're going to actually stomp on you if you express it."

—James Howard Kunstler, August 7, 2008
KunstlerCast #26: "From Hippies to Yuppies"

land parts, and the idea of living locally and living independently from the great corporate Moloch of America—not being dependent on all that stuff. That was a really healthy part of our culture, and it got an extended life—the Aquarian age segued into the OPEC oil embargo age in 1973. The hippie thing was still sort of going on, and a lot of those young people at that time got into solar energy and things that would have been useful if we had continued them. But unfortunately what we got instead was Reaganism and the idea that you could get everything and have everything and be everything. So a new consensus developed that you could have everything at once right now. And that developed into the yuppie kind of syndrome that I think you're describing.

DC: What happened? Why ditch it all for the suburbs?

JHK: One big element, of course, is that my generation was largely raised in suburbia, so they're just returning to the mean, returning to normal, which is a very common condition in many of the things of life—that they return to the mean after visiting the margin. It happens to the stock market, it happens to people's social behavior—returning to the norm.

The Baby Boomer generation was raised largely in the suburbs and became comfortable and accustomed to the comforts and conveniences of it. So it was easy for them to return to that as a living arrangement, especially when prompted by a number of incentives and disincentives in their practical life. For example, when my generation started reproducing, they were faced with the problem that the schools in the urban environments were bad schools. And that's a whole other area of discussion—why were they bad schools? We often gloss this over. It's not just because the kids were being taught badly by bad teachers, it was largely because of the behavior of the kids in the schools— they were out of control. They were being unkind and abusive and violent to their fellow students. This is not a milieu that any thoughtful person wants to subject their child to.

So, OK, what's the next step? You have to default to some other living arrangement, and as a practical matter that ends up being the suburbs in the 1970s, '80s and '90s in America. So my generation defaulted to that and they went out there. They didn't pay a whole lot of attention to the shortcomings and downsides of that choice—and the enabling device for that was the fact that the price of oil went down consistently after 1985 and made it more and more afford-able to live in that milieu. It removed the imperative for thinking about the alternatives that the hippies were thinking about in the late sixties and early seventies.

DC: What about the anti-war activi-ties? Was that a heroic moment in your generation's history?

JHK: The anti-war movement is not something that I would dismiss cava-lierly. It's hard to understand that, perhaps, without having been there, because it was for real. The war in Vietnam was a terrible thing. I would even go as far to say that it was more of a phony war than the Iraq war. As bad as it seems, you could actually see where our strategic interests lie in the Middle East a lot more easily than you could see where they were in Vietnam in 1967. And then there was the additional level of the draft problem where you had a lot of

people my age, in 1968, who didn't want to get conscripted into the army and sent twelve thousand miles away to get blown up and shot. This made people mad but it also created a lot of social inequity where the people like me, who were enrolled and matricu-lated in college programs, got a 2-S deferment and were not subject to the draft until they instituted the lottery in 1970.

When I went to the Democratic Convention in 1968, the draft was still on, the war was ramping up to its absolute height and its greatest level of craziness. Lyndon Johnson was still in the White House, and we were still being told that there was light at the end of the tunnel. And remem-ber, the casualties from the Vietnam War were way beyond what we see in Iraq. Over 50,000 Americans died in the Vietnam War. So far, a little more than 4,000 Americans have died in

Iraq and many more have been badly wounded. But Vietnam was a whole other level of death and violence.

So, yeah, that was the real deal and the protest against it was the realest part of the whole Aquarian revolution. Everything else going on around it—the oriental mysticism, the "Turn on, tune in, drop out" heavy drug scene—all that stuff was just sort of the icing on the cake. A lot of that, to me, was kind of disturbing.

DC: We're all by now familiar with Tom Brokaw's book *The Greatest Generation* and how he gave that moniker to the World War II generation. Do you think your generation is the "worst generation ever," which is an accusation floating around out there?

JHK: Well, I suppose I see them as being somewhere in between but verging more toward the disappointing end of the scale. Because we talked a really good game when we were twenty years old. And then all of a sudden we're out there buying Mercedes Benzes and McHouses and McMansions. We were queering the stock market, doing all these terrible things and running the United States into the ground. My generation, which climaxed with George W. Bush, has basically destroyed the United States. Yeah, we really did a bad job.

By the way, apropos of that, I would recommend the wonderful and underrated book *The Fourth Turning* by William Strauss and Neil Howe. It was a generational theory of history, as well as a discussion about the characteristics of generations within those cycles of history. One of the points they made is that the generation coming up in the early twenty-first century is going to inevitably *have* to be heroic. They will be faced with such enormous problems just as they come into full adulthood. And they are going to be like those 1940s type generations.

DC: Even though they were heroic, didn't the 1940s generation help create a lot of the problems that we're in now with suburbia and our cities, with the economy, with our oil dependency?

JHK: I have a very vivid sense of the entitlement of my parents' generation. For them, all the stuff that we take for granted—things ranging from happy motoring to air-conditioning on demand to every comfort that modern life has afforded us—for them it was the utmost normality, especially later in life. And part of that entitlement grew out of this World War II experience where "We paid such a price— we spent four of our years in the cane breaks of the Solomon Islands fighting the Japanese. Therefore, whatever these comforts are, we earned them and we're Number One and we're exceptional." They really bought into the Ronald Reagan fantasy of American exceptionalism, and, consequently, I think they set us up—their children—to do all the damaging things that we continue to do. I think both generations are very much at fault.

DC: That's a point that Michael Kinsley made in an article in *The Atlantic* magazine[25]—that you can also blame the parents of the Boomers for creating a mirage of prosperity and getting us addicted to debt and so on. But he went on to pose that, even though the Boomers do seem to have failed to live up to their ideals, it's not too late for them to make some grand gesture of selflessness for future generations.

JHK: I appreciate the guilt that underlies the wish or the idea. Behind this is obviously a tremendous generational guilt for having screwed up the planet. It's especially disgraceful considering our idealism of the 1960s, which ironically led to this disgraceful orgy of moneygrubbing of the late twentieth and early twenty-first centuries. It's been quite a transition for us Boomers and the one thing that I can imagine really happening—making sense—is that the Millennial generation will be so steamed by what we've done that they will simply deny us any elder care. "Forget about having operations and having a comfortable hospital bed when you're eighty years old Mr. Boomer, we're just gonna put you out on the curb like an old broken television and forget about you."

The Millennials will be heroic, but they'll also be perhaps a lot more hardheaded than we are. They're not going to have a therapeutic approach to everything in life and try to make everybody feel good. In fact, because we've destroyed their country, and perhaps their culture, they're not going to take care of us in our old age. We're going to be sitting there hoping to be put on the Medicare dole and be taken care of in nursing homes—having our bedpans changed when we're eighty-five years old. And the younger generation is going to say: "No. Sorry. You screwed up the world. We're just going to put you out in the street in a shopping cart. Good luck! And meanwhile, we're going to attend to all the disasters that you created by your incredible energy profligacy, your wastefulness, and the terrible choices that you made in your lifetime to impoverish the future."

DC: … Jim, I have a nice little shopping cart over here I'd like you to take a look at.

JHK: Would you just change my diapers before you put me in it, for God's sake?

Chapter 2: The End of Suburbia

Charging Our Way to Suburbia

Duncan Crary: So much of suburbia was bought on credit—the cars, the houses, the stuff to put in the houses. This all culminated in the economic crisis that's unfolding throughout the world now. When did we start buying everything on credit and how did that end up creating such an economic disaster?

James Howard Kunstler: It's an interesting phenomenon. It really begins in the 1920s when people are starting to get car loans or "install-ment loans"—you can make installment payments where you don't have to buy the whole thing up front. If a Ford Model T costs three hundred dollars, you can put down fifty dollars now, pay a half a dozen other payments of fifty dollars, and before you know it you're a car owner. That was all pretty straightforward and uncomplicated.

DC: And that's also how these new houses out in the burbs worked, too? You take a mortgage loan...

The Modern Mortgage and the Housing Bubble

JHK: Mortgages really started with the idea that you have this thing called your house which you've bought, but you need money, so you're going to put it up for collateral and get a loan against your house. That was the original idea of a mortgage—it was just a way of getting out of financial trouble using collateral.

But eventually it was turned into kind of a consumer device. You didn't have to just need cash to get a mortgage on your house. If you want to go out and buy a new house, you can do it on installment payments, which they eventually called a mortgage. In the beginning, you had to put up a substantial down payment—50 percent was expected when they first started in the US. And the term of the mortgage was pretty short, ten years or under.

But as we got comfortable with that as a culture—once we emerged from the Great Depression and the Second World War—you have a nation that's now attuned to the idea of a mortgage as being a normal thing. And we start to elaborate. The federal government gets in the act, especially where returning soldiers of World War II are concerned—they get various mortgage subsidies from the federal government.[1] And the whole thing becomes routinized and systematized so that the normal mortgage now is a thirty-year mortgage at 5 percent or 6 percent, and that becomes our basic reality for the next thirty, forty years.

Then we get into an interesting situation. We start to get rid of our manufacturing economy beginning in the 1970s, and the process accelerates through the eighties. A lot of people think we replaced manufacturing with the post-industrial digital informational economy or these other things that you call it. But that was never really true. Really, what we replaced the manufacturing economy with was a suburban sprawl/suburban house-building economy—that was the basis of it. As that occurred, it required more and more elaborate credit methods to continue the growth so that you got all kinds of new engineered mortgages, balloon mortgages, adjustable rate mortgages.

DC: This is how we created the housing bubble that just popped in 2008?

JHK: Right. So you get the bankers, and the homebuilders, and the appraisers, and the realtors, and the realtors' associations all conspiring to continue the racket of selling suburban homes and to elaborate this credit system. The unintended consequence of that is that they ramped up this horrendous bubble in suburban real estate—*in all real estate in the US*—including the accessories of suburban houses, which are the office parks, the commercial stuff, the strip malls, the power centers, the malls, etc. And we way overbuild all this stuff using credit.

The banks and the large financial institutions start to develop all these weird new engineered instruments and pathways for directing this mortgage money into strange places. There's a whole alphabet soup of these new things called "mortgage backed securities," "collateralized debt obligations," "structured investment vehicles," "credit default swaps." They all have little alphabetized nicknames. You know, SIVs and CDOs.

Ponzi Schemes and Hallucinated Wealth

DC: You might as well be speaking Martian to me right now.

JHK: The whole point of these things is that—rather than representing productive activity—they represent a sort of Ponzi scheme of getting something for nothing. Rather than representing the generation of real wealth, they represent swindles, basically, because they are not producing real wealth. But they seemed to for a while.

We do know that the mortgages that were bundled in these investments were, in many ways, swindles in and of themselves. They were contracts made with people who had no prospects of paying them back— people who lied about their incomes. The companies that originated these mortgages also behaved illegally themselves. They didn't do due diligence on their customers. They didn't check to see if their incomes were real or if they were really qualified for these mortgages. But they were raking in huge fees for collecting them, so it was to their advantage not to do due diligence.

All along the line—from the people who were applying for the mortgages, to the people who were giving them out, to the people who were bundling them and reselling them in tranches or bunches—there is a tremendous amount of fakery, and fraud, and people looking the other way, and people knowing they are doing the wrong thing, and, at the same time, generating enormous fees for all this. Pretty soon you've got a whole financial system that is totally out of control.

The mortgages were so dodgy—so many loans were given out to people with no hope of being able to pay back the debt—that they have to be foreclosed. That becomes an enormous problem because nobody knows where the mortgages really reside anymore. We found out as the systems started to come apart that mortgages of people in Freemont, California were owned by pension funds in Norway and all kinds of places all over the planet.

Then all the securities that were created by the banks start to blow up and go up in a vapor, and all the bad debt that that represents is simply going into a black hole—it's disappearing. It's going to a place where loaned money that is welshed on goes to, which is oblivion. So what you are seeing, really, is a huge amount of presumed wealth that is actually leaving the system.

And we are now going to be a poorer society, overbuilt for houses. The existing houses are losing their value at a very severe, steep rate, and the people who own them are in terrible trouble—they're "underwater" on their mortgages, as they say when the amount you owe on your mortgage is more than the value of your house. This has led to a fantastic fiasco.

By the way, similar things were going on in the car industry where you start to get car loans in which the payment schedule really exceeds the value of what the car is going to be worth before the payment schedule is over. For example, you get a forty-eight month loan on a Chevrolet and you're still paying for it in month forty-six and forty-eight, but by then the car's value is next to nothing.

The Great Bailout of 2008

DC: So with the bailout in 2008, the federal government steps in to back these bad mortgages. I can understand the goal to keep people in their homes. But why is the government also trying to prevent the value of all these homes from dropping? Why would our government intervene in that?

JHK: What we're seeing, in a way, is one manifestation of what I have identified as this campaign to sustain the unsustainable, which will extend to all the areas of contemporary life—the happy motoring realm and the retail blue light fiesta of shopping, and all the things that we associate with normality. There's going to be a tremendous attempt to keep the suburban system going at all costs, to rescue it all and prop it up.

There's a wish at many levels for the value of houses to stop sinking. But my guess is that nothing they can do will really stop it. I think that the prices will continue to go down no matter what happens. And I think the truth is that we shouldn't want it to stop, because it's very important to clear out all the clutter of unsold houses and to reach a point where the median price of a house is equal to the median income in America— because that's the baseline norm for how these things work. Until we get back to that point, this is just going to be an artificial process of attempting to prop up the price.

But events are really in the driver's seat now—not personalities and policies. And this thing is going to go where it needs to go regardless of what people, or governments, or institutions wish for it to do.

The Religion of Homeownership

DC: I can't help feeling like the trouble we've gotten into with the mortgage scandal and economic crisis has a lot to do with this almost religious dogma that says everyone in America needs to own his own house.

JHK: Well that's nonsense. It's kind of a nice sentimental thought, but in practice it just doesn't work out that way. There are an awful lot of people who, for one reason or another, probably shouldn't be in a house.

DC: They might be better off renting.

JHK: Of course!

DC: I'm an apartment renter, not a homeowner. People are always chiding me—"You're just throwing your money away on rent!"

JHK: Well, that's the rap. But the other idea is also proving to be fallacious—the idea that a home is necessarily an investment. It's not necessarily. A house is a place to live, which is also an article that you are buying that requires enormous amounts of reinvestment and maintenance on a regular basis. It was only in this weird period in the last ten years that we got the idea that buying houses was like buying IBM stock in 1957.

DC: I can't believe some of these houses out in suburbia are valued at half a million dollars. They're made of particleboard and plastic!

JHK: Yeah, I think we'll see quite a steep decline in the value of this stuff. We may even see a lot of older people on fixed incomes having to leave their property and move in with their children for one reason or another. People are going to be doubling up in households, which is only going to create a larger supply of unlived in, probably for-sale, houses. And we're going to see that this is going to turn into quite a downward spiral.

We're just not going to see the kind of orgy of mortgages and credit that we experienced in the last twenty years. We're done doing that.

There are an awful lot of shoes left to drop, though. As I said in one of my blogs, it's going to sound like the All American Clog Dance out there because so many shoes are going to be dropping.

Feeling Vindicated

DC: Jim, you've been saying for years that building suburbia was the greatest misallocation of resources in human history. Do you feel somewhat vindicated by the housing bubble collapse and the economic crisis it caused?

JHK: Oh God, I don't have any kind of real moment-by-moment conscious sense of gloating about anything. I'm too busy to really get off on that.

DC: You don't see this economic collapse as payback to all these idiots who've been driving SUVs around and living in McMansions?

JHK: Well, I'm not—I don't feel vengeful about it, you know, like some character out of a Tony Soprano drama trying to whack his adversaries. The way I feel about it is that we have a manner of life that produces a tremendous amount of discomfort, distress, unhappiness, anxiety, depression, hardship, violence. And when circumstances compel us to live differently we're going to benefit hugely from making these changes... from getting away from a lot of the habits and practices that we've been engaged in.

The New Urbanism

Duncan Crary: Jim, you never formally studied urban planning or architecture. How do you respond to the practitioners who try to discredit your analysis of suburbia because you don't have a planning or design degree?

James Howard Kunstler: Well, it's certainly fair for people to wonder what my credentials are. I mean, I'm mouthing off about these things and here are all these planners with credentials—they resent it. I understand that.

But it's pretty obvious that the kind of training that so-called urban planners have gotten over the last fifty years has included almost nothing about real urban design. And certainly nothing about the real historical methodologies of how to construct and assemble a human habitat that's worth being in.

Mostly they get trained in statistical analysis, and traffic engineering, and mitigation of water runoff. These are issues that are not unimportant. But given the kind of education the professionals received—look at the environments they created. Look at how awful they are to be in. Look at how unpleasant and fearful they are. Think of children having to be on an eight-lane highway on the shoulder on their bicycle going to Baskin-Robbins from their housing subdivision. Was that a great job of urban design? I don't think so. They disgraced their profession and they deserve all the opprobrium that is being heaped on them.

DC: Would you describe yourself as a generalist?

JHK: I suppose, in terms of the books I've written about cities and suburbs.

DC: It sounds like you're reluctant to be labeled a generalist.

JHK: I'm reluctant to be labeled anything—a doom-and-gloomer, a hippie… If I have to define myself as one, I would say that I am a generalist by default, because I never went to graduate school, and I was never certified in any particular discipline. I just rambled and blundered and lurched around as a young person. My college experience had nothing really to do with what I do in professional life. My pathway was from college to journalism.

Just by happenstance, I ended up not being certified. I wasn't an architect. I wasn't an urban designer, thank God probably. All I was, was a writer. But I was interested in certain things and I had to educate myself. I don't consider myself a great expert in any of these disciplines. I consider my strong point to be prose composition.

DC: You do have some thoughts on the built environment and the direction our civilization is heading in that are unique, though—that you express through your prose.

JHK: I don't know that they're unique. They're thoughts that are—at the moment—counter to the conventional wisdom of my culture and counter to the practices and habits of my culture, and with our physical surroundings and the places where we live. These are things that have concerned me ever since I became an adult and became aware of being dissatisfied with the places that I had to live in—whether it was Boston, Massachusetts, or the suburb that I spent three years in as a kid, or the Manhattan that I knew in 1964, or the

Small Town USA that I've lived in for thirty years.

The Dangers of Hyper-Specialization

DC: Do you feel that the urban planning profession needs more generalists?

JHK: Perhaps another way to approach that is to look at the danger of hyper-specialization. Our culture is getting hammered from hyper-specialists who are absolutely wonderful at what they do and disregardful of the larger picture. So you get a lot of preoccupation with stuff that has nothing to do with how we feel about the places that we live in and whether we care about them, and whether they really provide a dwelling place for us to have a civilized life.

The hyper-specialization that has gone on in American graduate schools and in the professional planning practice in the last fifty years has been so extreme that there are very few generalists out there who are even willing to look at the big picture. You have the parking experts who are only concerned with car storage—they don't care about what the quality of the street is like outside of their parking structures. You have the municipal officials who end up being more concerned with economic development issues—which themselves are perverted because they tend to involve national chain stores, or chain hotels, or convention center schemes. That whole economic development field is full of "voodoo" economics.

Probably the exemplar of all this are the traffic engineers, who are solely concerned with the geometry of the turns and banking the freeway ramps. They don't care about what your experience is in the city of Milwaukee or Oklahoma City—all they care about is taking care of the cars, and they have these exquisitely fine-tuned formulas for doing what they do. They can build highways with all the right curve ratios and grades. They can design streets that move huge numbers of cars flawlessly through places. But as they do that, they tend to screw up our cities and towns pretty badly.

You go to a place—whether it's Providence or Minneapolis or St. Louis—and there's always some set of important streets that have been turned into four-laners or six-laners in the heart of town. They've removed the parallel parking. They've made them one-way so that the cars can move with great efficiency through the city. And you end up with a street that's dead and a neighborhood that's dead, because it's composed of nothing but one-way, four-lane streets. So the traffic engineers have done their job and carried out their specialty exactly as they have been commissioned and directed to do, and they've ended up destroying the city.

We're entering a new period, though, where it's not going to just be about water mitigation and handling traffic, and counting the number of so-called consumers who pass from point A to point B on a given day. We're going to have to return to methodologies that were lost, and that's one of the reasons that I was so attracted to the New Urbanists. Because these were people who realized that their training was inadequate. They'd come out of the architecture schools and the urban planning schools, and realized they knew nothing about designing and assembling places that were rewarding to be in.

The New Urbanists

DC: Tell me about the New Urbanist movement. What is New Urbanism? How did it get started?

JHK: What happened was a bunch of Boomer-generation architects and planners, even developers, started to realize that the built environment in the United States was such a fiasco—and it was getting worse, and it was going on a track that was going to take it in really dangerous directions of total unsustainability. Americans were building places that had no future, that people hated, that oppressed them in every way and punished them for living in them. The New Urbanists knew we had to build places that were better than the crappy suburban environments we were coming up with.

These were some well-intentioned, well-educated, smart, savvy people. In a way they were the best of their generation. The New Urbanists included people like Andrés Duany, one of the founders of New Urbanism—a fabulously interesting and rather heroic figure in this field and in our culture—and his wife Elizabeth Plater-Zyberk, who went on to become the dean of the University of Miami School of Architecture, one of the few really great schools of urban design in America now. And Peter Calthorpe out in Berkeley and Doug Kelbaugh, who was at the University of Washington at the time. And a lot of very cool people. The list is very long.

They dove into the garbage can of history and they started looking around for the stuff that we had thrown away in our zeal to become a suburban nation. They read Vitruvius[2] and read Hegemann and Peets's great civic art compendium[3] from the 1920s. They visited the places where people still lived in wonderful habitats. And they measured things—the early New Urbanists were freaks for measurement. They would go to a European town and they would measure the heights of the curbs and the distance between the shop front and the street, and how big the medians were, and the ground floors of the buildings—where the transition lines began, and the depth of the balconies and the porticoes.

They discovered all these principles and ways of building things that had tremendous value and that would allow us to actually get back on a different track of building places that were worth living in—places that had a future, places that were, to use the cliché of the day, "sustainable," in the sense that they weren't built to be thrown away or trashed and didn't have to be radically transformed every nine years when the economy changed. They realized they had to reestablish what the parameters were going to be for creating an environment that people wanted to be in.

They found some partners in the other parts of the American economy—namely the developers and the bankers—who would go along with them in building these new kinds of things, which came in the form of whole new towns like Seaside in Florida. A lot of people saw Seaside and they thought, "You know, gosh, we can do this in other parts of the country. You can build this in Iowa, and Connecticut, and New Jersey, and North Carolina." And during this whole period from the late

1980s on, we entered this incredible last orgasm of the cheap energy era, which was also the cheap-and-easy credit era. So there was an awful lot of money to finance these things, and there was a lot of work for these guys.

Andrés Duany and his wife Elizabeth Plater-Zyberk—and their firm DPZ—they're really the leaders in this kind of work in America. Their work is wonderful.

Seaside

Duncan Crary: Why is Seaside important?

James Howard Kunstler: Seaside was the original, iconic demonstration project of the New Urbanism. It became in many ways the model for what the Traditional Neighborhood Development would be.

Originally when the owner and developer of the property, Robert Davis, first hired Andrés Duany and Liz Plater-Zyberk and a bunch of other architects, the idea they started with was that this would be a kind of Bohemian beach town where artists and architects would come together, and it wouldn't be so grand. It was just about eighty acres on the seacoast, in a desolate corner of the Florida Panhandle between Panama City and Pensacola. It never had any pretensions to be anything other than a beach town.

But as it began to get built out, the quality of it was so outstanding that it became recognized almost overnight as prime real estate. It attracted the attention of orthopedic surgeons from Birmingham, Alabama, and wealthy lawyers from Tallahassee....

Developers from Atlanta started buying property there. They bid up the prices of not just the buildings, but the empty lots.

So it was a fabulously success-ful project. But I think what people miss is that the really great achievement of these New Urbanists was not necessarily just building a successful real estate venture—or even a new

At Seaside

At Seaside, all the houses are made of wood with peaked tin roofs and deep porches. No two are alike, but all share a congruity of design that is soothing to eyeballs scalded by the chaotic squalor of the strip. The pastel-colored houses stand along a coherent network of narrow streets paved with brick. Cars parked parallel-wise line the streets, as they might in any small town. Otherwise, there are no parking lots or special accommodation for cars. Picket fences enclose small front yards. At the center of the town stands a grocery store, an open-air market, a couple of beer joints, an upscale eatery—no illuminated plastic signs, thank you—and a little Greek temple-style post office. At spacious intervals along the crest of the dunes stand three columned pavilions with graceful wooden steps leading down to the Gulf of Mexico. They look like gateways to the sea, which is just what they are—it's that simple.

—James Howard Kunstler
The Geography of Nowhere [4]

town—but proving that something new could be wonderful. America had been conditioned so profoundly for half a century to believe that every new thing is horrible. Because Americans had lost faith that anything new that was built would be any good. Their expectation was "It'll be just another piece of crap that will make my life worse and make my property worse and devalue my home," whether it's a strip mall or a housing development. And Seaside demonstrated that you could produce something new from the ground up that would be a wonderful human artifact and a wonderful place to live.

It had a lot of lessons for the public and for the architecture profession. Although I'd say by-and-large the architecture profession disdained it for its traditionalism. It just wasn't cutting-edge enough for them. It didn't confound our sensibilities enough for them. It catered too much to making people feel OK in their surroundings, and that's a no-no in the architecture racket these days.

Seaside as the Emblem of Unreality?

DC: What are some other complaints about Seaside?

JHK: Seaside eventually took on some unreal characteristics. It became overpriced. And, to some extent, Robert Davis operated part of the project as a deconstructed hotel, partly because they wanted to get people down to see it and how it operated. Instead of having a big hotel building, his property office would lease out or rent individual houses or parts of houses to vacationers who had access to the town center and amenities like the community pool. So people drew the conclusion that it was phony. But most of the real estate in Seaside actually ended up being either private houses or small businesses, restaurants, shops.

The other thing was that over the years Seaside was criticized for being "elitist." That was always strange to me, because it's as though the people who were criticizing it expected it to turn out to be a Welsh coal-mining town, or a United Auto Workers vacation spot, or something that it wasn't. It was a beach town. Of course, people didn't live there year round— it was their vacation town—just like a lot of people don't live on Martha's Vineyard all year round. The funny thing was that a lot of the so-called right-thinking progressives—exactly the type of people who have places on Martha's Vineyard—would dis Seaside. They were the people who seemed to be disappointed that it didn't turn out to be some working-class construction of some kind. If you delve into that just a couple of centimeters, you realize it's the elitists complaining that other people are elitist.

DC: Many people might not recognize Seaside by name, but they've seen it if they've watched *The Truman Show*, because it was the filming location for that movie.

JHK: Oh sure. And it suffered from that for years. That was the emblem of unreality that was stuck on it.

DC: In the movie, Jim Carrey played a character who was living in a giant sound stage, and the entire town was fake, and all the people in the town were actors in a reality TV show.

JHK: And he didn't know it.

DC: He didn't know. He was the only one who didn't know he was being filmed the whole time for reality TV. That was all shot in Seaside. I've only seen the place in pictures and in

The Truman Show. But from what I've seen, it seems a little bit.... I wouldn't want to live in Seaside.

JHK: It's actually a very wonderful place, though there are elements of it that make it unreal. As I said, it's a vacation town—

DC: But it's not just the vacation town aspect that makes it seem unreal to some people. I have a quote of yours from *The Geography of Nowhere* about your own impressions of Seaside: "At first, one catches a fugitive whiff of theme park cutesiness on the balmy sea breeze." Then you go on to write: "If Seaside seems a little too perfect, it is only because everything there is so spanking new."[5] So there's a newness about the place that makes some people feel like it isn't real.

JHK: Seaside was all built within about a fifteen-year period. You could say the same thing about Cape May, New Jersey, or about Oak Bluffs on Martha's Vineyard. These are places that were also built out within a short period of time.

But when Seaside was first built—and with other new towns that the New Urbanists were then undertaking—people were complaining that they were no good because they were all new. And Andrés Duany had to remind them that when you're making an omelet, you can take the eggs and the onions and green peppers and the cheese and put them in a bowl, but you wouldn't serve them that way. You actually have to cook the ingredients a little while to produce the omelet. A town has to cook for a while, too.

It takes a long time for all these little individual decisions to modify things and change things. The house that was originally built to be a high-classical Greco-Roman building will eventually take on other characteristics. Some people will take better care of their property. Some people will take worse care of their property. Some of these places will become the rundown corners of the village or the hamlet. Some will remain the great parts.

Criticisms of New Urbanism

DC: I've heard other criticisms of New Urbanism that seem to have merit to a guy like me, who lives in and loves old cities. A lot of the New Urbanist projects are located out in suburbia. And even though these new neighborhoods follow good urban principles, you're still dependent on the car.

JHK: The New Urbanists are often criticized for the greenfield developments that they did, which is to say they were built on so-called undeveloped land, in pastures and cornfields. I understand that criticism. The New Urbanists, in recent years, became hostages of the production home-building industry, and they hitched themselves to the methods and practices and financing increments of that industry.

They may not agree with me, but a lot of their projects were essentially much better suburbs than the conventional subdivisions—the so-called Traditional Neighborhood Developments were greenfield developments. But they attempted to do them better. They attempted to incorporate town centers. Another thing the New Urbanists tried very hard to do was to accommodate the automobile in a way that wouldn't wreck the public space in these places. They took great pains to accommodate the car wherever possible because they saw that overcoming the American dependence on and love for cars would be impossible. So they did everything possible to accommodate, but still discipline, the car—to store it in places where it would be unobtrusive, to allow for on-street parking, to get the garages off the front of the house.

DC: To build alleyways…

JHK: To build alleyways and lanes to put the garage on. But when all was said and done they were left with the essential paradox of contributing to more ex-urban development, which required people to drive.

DC: Maybe you could say they were building neighborhoods on training wheels… Trying to reintroduce people to living in better places—

JHK: That's a good way of putting it.

DC: That's probably why I grapple with the term: am I a "New Urbanist"? I don't think I necessarily am. I think I'm just an "urbanist."

JHK: "New Urbanist" as a concept, in some ways, only really had meaning in opposition to the suburbanists or to the conventional suburban scheme and methodology. Now that the conventional suburban guys are biting the dust, so to speak, the New Urbanism really becomes just good urbanism, or urbanism per se.

DC: After reading your latest book, *The Long Emergency*, I wanted to ask if you've given up on the New Urbanism?

JHK: I haven't given up on the New Urbanism at all. If anything, the New Urbanists were among the reformers who had the most comprehensive and kindest vision of a possible positive outcome for the set of changes we're heading into.

But for a number of reasons, I don't think we're going to see much more of their stock and trade of the last fifteen years—the Traditional Neighborhood Development running about four hundred acres, built out in a cornfield or cow pasture.

The New Urbanist movement was, in part, an attempt to compromise with the habits and practices of America. I viewed them for a long time as being a transitional movement between where we were at in the late twentieth century and where we're going. On the whole, I think the New Urbanists did a pretty good job, given what their aim was. But still it doesn't get to the heart of the matter, which is that reality is not going to let us live in the suburban manner anymore—whether they're good suburbs or better suburbs or really, really great suburbs. We're done with that.

I view a lot of those projects that the New Urbanists did—the new neighborhoods and towns that were built in the suburban areas—as being kind of transitional forms. They were places that had to make the leap between the automobile age and whatever follows, and they didn't make the complete leap. Some of these places may have a brighter destiny than the conventional subdivisions—places like Kentlands and Seaside, and there are a couple in the Carolinas that are pretty good. It depends on where they are geographically in relationship to public transit and the cities or the towns that are nearby.

But they were a compromise. And I know the New Urbanists compromised strenuously when it came to doing hybrid projects. Like when they attempted to retrofit shopping malls for town centers. There were quite a few of those done in the last twenty years. They always included massive amounts of structured parking and careful attention to providing parking spaces on the streets. It was all about parking, because no matter how you cut it, even if you wanted to design a really great street or a really great neighborhood, at that point in history you just couldn't get away from the public consensus that the car was indispensable. The American public could not imagine not having a car or not having to deal with it and not having to store it and park it. So the New Urbanists bent over backwards to accommodate the car and they still produced good work.

I admire them a lot for doing what they could with what they had to work with. But the reality that we're presented with now is quite a bit different. That will involve moving back into truly traditional neighborhoods and towns that are not going to be dominated by the car, and in which the automobile is simply not going to be as much of a presence as it has been. I think that will be a good thing in a lot of ways.

But it also points to the fact that in some ways we're going to be a more austere society in a more difficult economy.

The Next New Urbanists

DC: What's the next phase for the New Urbanists?

JHK: We're certainly going to be doing things differently in the decades ahead. If nothing else, the scale of the way that we build things and assemble them is going to be much more modest because we're going to be a less affluent society. We're going to have less energy to indulge in. We are not going to be able to traverse these pharaonic distances. And that's going to influence the next generation of people who get into urban design. They're already out there. I meet them in my travels—many of them are members of the Congress for the New Urbanism, the official professional society of the New Urbanists.

A lot of these young people have very laboriously self-educated themselves in the things that they're not getting in their schools. And they come into this cohort of people who think similarly. They get a lot more training from the older guys who are around. But the economies of scale that those first New Urbanists enjoyed are disappearing now along with a lot of other economic relationships that are leaving our society and our economy. I saw evidence of it at a recent Congress for the New Urbanism, when I met several architects who were very unhappy at the fact that their work was drying up.

But the real achievement of the New Urbanists was not building the projects like Seaside. It was retrieving that important principle and methodology for understanding how to design and assemble real towns and real cities. And I think that it will now be applied to the existing small cities and towns, in places like Troy, where you live. It's already happening in Saratoga. And increasingly, that will be the case. The increment in development will be smaller. Instead of doing these four-hundred-acre new town projects, we'll be lucky if we can do a new intersection or a new corner in a town, or a new block—or, for that matter, one or two really good building lots on a block.

DC: You think New Urbanism is going to be about filling in the gaps in our cities—the parking lots and vacant spaces—and fixing up the old downtowns?

JHK: I do think that our towns and *small* cities are going to redevelop. But it may be a much more haphazard process going forward, especially in the years directly ahead, because we're going to be really hard up for money.

In the Great Depression of the 1930s, the industry that was hit the hardest was the construction industry, and very little was built of any kind. The suburban ventures that were begun in the 1920s during the boom pretty much ceased, and not a whole lot was done in the cities, which became kind of rundown in that ten-year period which adjoined another five years of the Second World War.

DC: So how do you see the architecture profession changing as this recession rolls on?

JHK: We don't know whether the architects will be brought into the program in the future. Because under the best circumstances it's fine to have architects and buildings that are designed by people who really know how to design them. But it's also more expensive to build that way, and you might just see builders. Or what you might see is that the profession itself changes so that architects have to do the building themselves. They may have to become the contractors, as was the case in early nineteenth-century America.

In fact, a lot of the great domestic architecture of early America was done by guys who were builder-designers. They had a tremendous amount of skill, and they actually collected their knowledge in books like the building companion books that every carpenter knew about. This included a lot of really arcane information about things like proportioning Greco-Roman columns and how to do the returns on the gable ends and all those things, which most builders don't know how to do correctly anymore. I think that skill may be reorganized with the business of designing and building, so that we end up getting builders who have more skills—who for all practical purposes are architects. What the architects probably won't be doing is designing a lot of forty-story condo skyscrapers and lifestyle centers and malls.

DC: Jim, do you consider yourself to be a "New Urbanist?"

JHK: I *am* a New Urbanist, and I am in pretty thoroughgoing agreement with their principles.

DC: How do you define your role in the New Urbanist movement?

JHK: I've just been part of that process as a journalist, really. And I've absorbed a tremendous amount of information and methodology. I have to add, I don't practice as a consultant in urban design and when people ask me to, I make a real point of saying that's beyond my competence. I'm not a professional consultant and I don't ask to be paid for it. I will come to a university or to a civic organization and I'll give a speech or a talk, or I will inveigh against their past practices. But I don't fob myself off as a practicing urban designer.

From Suburban Sprawl to Peak Oil

Duncan Crary: You have what you call a "Long Emergency" view of where civilization is heading. What is "The Long Emergency?"

James Howard Kunstler: I've labeled this situation we're heading into "The Long Emergency" because I think it's going to be a protracted experience for mankind and for us in the United States in particular. It's really about how we are heading into a period of resource scarcity and the disruption and depletion of our oil supplies. It's about the allocation of this crucial resource all around the world, and the geopolitical implications of those inequities. And how these problems are going to combine with climate change to cause problems with everything we do, from how we produce and distribute our food to how we're going to have trade and manufacturing when Walmart dies. And not least, the destiny of the suburban, car-dependent, happy motoring living arrangement. Which is probably, for me, the biggest part of the equation.

DC: And you don't see good things in store for the suburbs in the Long Emergency?

JHK: Suburbia is going to fail a lot worse than it's already failing, because we're not going to have the energy to run it the way it's been designed to run. For that reason I refer to suburbia as the greatest misallocation of resources in the history of the world. We took all of our post-world war wealth—and actually quite a bit of the wealth that we had accumulated for decades before that—and we invested it in this living arrangement that had no future. And now we're stuck with it. And to make matters worse, we didn't build it very well in the first place. So as it begins to decay it decays very rapidly and becomes a very unrewarding place to live in.

DC: Jim, it seems almost impossible to persuade suburbanites that there's anything wrong with suburbia or that it could ever "fail." I've tried, and it almost feels like arguing with someone about deeply held religious beliefs.

JHK: Again, one of the unfortunate repercussions of building suburbia, is: now that we've built it, it provides a very powerful psychology of previous investment. Which means that you put so much of your wealth into this system already—into this structure for daily life with no future—and you've invested so much of your national identity in it, that you can't even imagine letting go of it or substantially changing it or reforming it. And that, I believe, is what's behind our inability to have a coherent discussion about what we're going to do about our problems in America. Because the psychology of previous investment has got us trapped in a box—we will not allow ourselves to think about how we're going to do without this crap.

DC: You give lots of reasons in *The Long Emergency* and in your other writings for why suburbia is going to fail. But the biggest one is that suburbia only works when you have a cheap fossil fuel supply, and you say that supply of cheap fuel is running out. How do you counter the "Drill, Baby, Drill" camp? The folks who believe there are "Saudi Arabias" of oil right here in the US just waiting to come out of the ground?

JHK: There's this general misunderstanding that there are huge amounts of oil reserves in and around North America that are waiting to be exploited. North America is one of the most thoroughly explored regions on the Earth for oil and we pretty much know what's down there. And when you hear people saying we gotta "drill, drill, drill" for ANWR—well, I was never even against drilling in ANWR, the Arctic National Wildlife Refuge. My idea was that Obama should get behind it just to disarm the stupid Republicans so they wouldn't keep yakkin' about it, because there's such an insignificant amount of oil up there.

DC: What about the tar sands, shale gas and shale oil?

JHK: A lot of people think we're going to compensate our losses elsewhere. But the tar sands will probably never produce more than three million barrels a day. And I think we *will* discover a lot of gas trapped in that tight rock. But that's very expensive and difficult to get out.

There is also a lot of wishful thinking about switching our truck fleet over to natural gas, because we have "a hundred years" or "three hundred years" of natural gas.[6] That's just not true. All of these ideas and programs aren't going to work out the way we wish they would, because so much of this is about wishful thinking and fantasy. Look, we use twenty million barrels of oil a day in the USA. And what we're talking about here are very expensive mining operations,

Climate Change

The problems of climate change are going to ramify the problems of our energy predicament and vise versa—they're going to mutually reinforce each other and amplify all the problems associated with both of them. The coming permanent oil crisis is going to change everything about how we live, and we're sleepwalking into the future.

—James Howard Kunstler, February 10, 2010 lecture hosted by the Stakeholders, at Sage College, Albany, New York which also happen to be fantastically environmentally destructive.

DC: In the past few years, you've become increasingly focused on how our financial problems may be a more immediate catalyst for the Long Emergency than energy.

JHK: It was kind of a surprising thing. Many of us who were following the oil problem and the energy predicament over the last ten years, we thought the situation would come to a head over energy supplies and prices. And in a way they did. But really the salient effect of all that was that we destroyed the banking system. The net effect of that right now is that the USA is broke at all levels — including the household level at the bottom, the corporate enterprise level in the middle and the government level at the top — and that includes all levels of the government: federal, state, county and munici-

pal. We're all broke at every level. We don't have money at our disposal any more so we're going to have to figure out some other strategies for creating a post-fossil fuel economy, for carrying our civilization forward, for enabling us to remain civilized.

From *The Geography of Nowhere* to *The Long Emergency*

Duncan Crary: Tell me how you got from *The Geography of Nowhere* to *The Long Emergency*. When did you first start thinking about the connection between oil depletion and the fate of suburban sprawl?

James Howard Kunstler: I guess we'd have to really go back to the 1970s. I had come from the hippie newspapers in Boston and I had just gotten a full-time job on the evening paper in Albany, New York.[7] The newspaper had just established itself in a brand new building on this heroic boulevard of strip shopping, about ten miles outside of Albany. It had moved from a building downtown out to the suburbs.

I got there in August of 1973, and about three months later, we got into the OPEC oil embargo. It was a huge local story everywhere, but it was pretty severe in our region. A lot of the gas stations were not getting gas, and there were lines at the gasoline stations everywhere—tempers were flaring, people were beating each other up, guns were brandished.

The whole thing only lasted a couple of months. I think the worst of it only ran about three or four weeks. But for that time, there were very few people driving, if they could possibly avoid it. The highways were empty. The streets were empty. It was like *The Day the Earth Stood Still*.

It made a huge impression on me, because here I was a young reporter—about twenty-five years old or so—and I saw the world-as-we-had-known-it stop. It was especially peculiar seeing this happen in the new burgeoning suburbia, as it was being built out and elaborated. So it made a huge impression on me: "This is important—how we live in America and what it's going to mean for how we get to where we're going in the future in America. I've seen a little glimpse of the future now and I wonder what's going to be happening." And then it was over. It came to an end.

It did provoke a lot of changes and troubles for the rest of the decade. We had an economy that was badly upset by oil prices that rose very quickly, very steeply. We had stagflation, which was a new phenomenon that nobody had ever seen before, where you have inflation plus a stagnating economy. You began to see the American manufacturing sector fall apart. The first manifestation was when the Japanese carmakers started to get the upper hand over Ford and General Motors. The American carmakers were all tooled up to build these giant cars the size of ferry boats, and in comes Nissan, and Honda, and Datsun, as it was called at the time—they're selling cars that are three feet shorter, and use one-third of the amount of gas, and all of a sudden the Americans are buying them like crazy. You saw all kinds of other changes going on.

I moved on in the meantime. I went to *Rolling Stone* for a while. Then came back to Saratoga to embark on my Bohemian adventure as a novel writer. I wrote a whole bunch of novels. They all got published by major trade publishers, although I wouldn't exactly call them successful. I would get advances. But it was just not enough money to live on. So I returned to nonfiction and journalism.

The New York Times Magazine sent me out on a bunch of stories about suburban development in New England, because a lot of the editors owned summer houses in Vermont and Massachusetts and they were getting hip to the idea that the countryside was getting "overdeveloped" as they would put it.

Why is America So Fucking Ugly?

JHK: One article that I was writing was called "Why is America So Fucking Ugly?" That was sort of the working title between the editors and me. That wouldn't have been the title they published but that's how we understood the theme, because the most obvious manifestation of what we were doing and how we were building America was that it was ugly.

The story was killed, not because of the title but because they had instituted a new rule at the *Times* that the stories could not exceed 4,000 words. This one went way over that and there was no way of even touching on the subject in less. So I took that story that was killed and turned it into a book proposal which sold pretty rapidly.

It wasn't a huge contract but it was more money than I had made before. The working title of the book was going to be *Scary Places* because America was getting scary and to me it was inducing placeaphobia. Because all of a sudden there are all these places you don't want to be in anymore. They are just so horrifying. So "Scary Places" was written. It took me about three years. They decided they didn't like the title because it sounded too much like a horror novel.

DC: Or a book for three-year-olds…

JHK: Yeah, like *Where the Wild Things Are* or something. So I just switched around the title of the first chapter with the title of the book. The first chapter became "Scary Places" and the title became *The Geography of Nowhere.*

In that book, I was touching upon the idea that sooner or later we were going to run into problems with oil. I based that on this experience I'd had, as a young man, of the OPEC oil embargo, and knowing the proportion of oil we imported would only go up and become ever larger and it would become ever more of a threat and a problem for us. Here's one passage, for example:

Even after 1990, when the savings and loan catastrophe left the commercial real estate market in shambles, and the American economy began to slide into a malaise resembling the Great Depression, developers were still building some major projects in the same old foolish manner: single-family detached homes on half-acre lots out in the hills, minimalls along the connector roads, accountant's offices out in the old cornfields. But these are the mindless twitchings of a brain-dead culture, artificially sustained by the intravenous feeding of cheap oil. Indeed, the continuation of a cheap oil supply through the 1980s—a temporary quirk of politics and history—has been a disaster, allowing us to postpone the necessary redesign of America.[8]

So you can sort of see the ways things were shaping up out there. What I didn't realize was that the North Sea discoveries and the Alaska Prudhoe Bay discoveries would extend that cheap oil interlude through the nineties. In fact, oil got just cheaper and cheaper.

What happened was the North Sea and Alaska took the leverage away from OPEC and other oil-producing nations who didn't like us.

DC: So peak oil was something you were thinking about even back when you were writing *The Geography of Nowhere*?

JHK: I wouldn't say that I was thinking of things with that term "peak oil." The way I thought of it at that time was we have an oil import problem that is just going to get worse and worse. Indeed it has. My understanding of peak oil came about a different way. I went on to write a sequel to *The Geography of Nowhere* called *Home from Nowhere*, published in 1996. That book was largely a result of my meeting the New Urbanists, the guys who were the real reformers out there in the urban design, architecture, town planning fields. I started hanging out with them a lot. They were so interesting and stimulating and intelligent. I just got such a bang out of seeing what they proposed as a remedy for this crazy way of life we developed. It was hugely stimulating to find these guys.

Home from Nowhere was concerned with the remedies to suburbia in terms of urban design and architecture. Really, how we were going to rebuild the human habitat in a way that would have a future that would be sustainable, that would be more rewarding to be in.

Peak Oil

JHK: Around the same time that *Home from Nowhere* was published, in the mid-1990s, a group of senior geologists started retiring out of the oil industry. As soon as they established their pensions safely and retired into comfort, they started to publish their secret, dark thoughts about where the oil industry was headed. These were characters like Colin J. Campbell and Kenneth Deffeyes. Deffeyes had been a Texaco geologist who then went on to Princeton and became an academic. Colin J. Campbell worked for the European companies, Total and some others.

What they were saying was: "Here we are in the mid 1990s. We know, from the models that our teachers in geology devised before us in the 1950s and '60s, that there is a certain profile to the oil story—that it has a beginning, a middle and an end. And we're going to call this the peak oil story." The model was mostly devised by this one particular guy, Marion King Hubbert, who was an industry geologist and an academic. He was at Columbia. He was at the Colorado School of Mines. He worked for a number of the major oil companies. He devised what came to be called the Hubbert Curve, which is a bell curve that says: "The oil industry starts and you are producing very little. Then you are ramping it up. The curve goes up and you are producing a whole lot. Then you reach a certain point of maximum all-time production, and from there you enter the arc on the other side of the bell curve. That's the Arc of Depletion. That is how the oil story will play out. It will probably begin to peak in the late 1990s or early 2000s."

Hubbert lived until 1989. So his career spanned a very long time, from the infancy of the oil industry to near peak. He called it pretty well. One of the things he was famous for calling was that America had already gone through its peak in 1970. That was the year we produced the most oil that we will ever produce. It was something like ten million barrels a day. Now we're down to under five. Our production had peaked in 1970, which you could see through the rearview mirror by looking at the production figures from '71, '72 and '73.

It began to be evident that we could not produce more oil than we had in 1970. It not only became obvious to us and to our engineers and our military people, etc., it also became known internationally. We needed it so badly, we were getting it from the guys overseas. So all of a sudden we're deathly dependent on them. And when the OPEC nations figured it out, they seized the pricing control.

Mr. Hubbert had also gone on to model the global oil peak and the beginning of global depletion. He predicted 1995 would be the beginning of this. He was off by a few years. It now appears that we produced the most conventional crude oil ever in 2005 and haven't really exceeded it.

DC: Do you think it's a widely accepted fact that 2005 was the global oil peak?

JHK: I think there's a general understanding from looking at the figures that—at least since 2005—we have entered what we call the bumpy plateau period, which is how the peak looks close up. If you looked at the tip of a hypodermic needle under a strong microscope you would see that it is not exactly smooth. It has little imperfections in it. Well, the tippy top of the peak of oil is not totally smooth either. It's composed of little bumps and that's where we have been at for the last few years or so. But we are getting a lot of signals that we are now entering the robust period of depletion.

So these guys like Campbell and Deffeyes retired out of the system and started to publish their thoughts about where the oil industry was headed. That was about 1996. It was still a rather esoteric issue. It certainly wasn't being discussed in the mainstream media or even in the most esoteric journals, really. The intellectual places like *The Atlantic Monthly* and *Harpers*, they weren't really talking about it either.

But the Internet was starting to ramp up around that time. And peak oil was a subject that was coming up on the Internet, along with, by the way, Y2K. These are two interesting phenomena that the media weren't really paying much attention to. One of them, Y2K, turned out to be a problem that was solved because it was a very specific, limited problem.

It was a large problem but it was limited and specific.

The Geopolitics of Peak Oil

JHK: The peak oil problem, the more you looked at it, presented really horrendous implications for us. The biggest one being: how is an industrial society going to run itself when we run into a supply problem with oil? Hand-in-hand with that went the idea that oil is not distributed equitably around the world—it tends to be in certain places and not in other places. Unfortunately, some of the places that have the most oil are the places that we don't get along with very well, namely the Islamic world and Russia.

So that problem stimulated the geopolitical issues of peak oil. A lot of these issues were self-explanatory. You didn't have to be a PhD to understand that if 75 percent of the oil in the world was controlled by people who didn't like the United States, and if you combine that with the idea that production is peaking in the whole world, then this doesn't bode very well for how we're going to get on—especially in relation to a society that has completely been sucked into car dependence of the most extreme kind, that has created an entire living arrangement based on car dependency, which represents the investment of all of its post–World War II wealth in the strip malls and the housing tracts and all of the equipment of daily life. You can see in the swirl of all these issues a very disturbing picture beginning to present itself.

DC: So the peak oil story came onto your radar in the mid-1990s. But you wouldn't really start writing about it extensively in *The Long Emergency* for a few years still. What about your third book, *The City in Mind*—were you influenced by the idea of peak oil while you were writing that?

JHK: I published *The City in Mind* in 2002 while I was being exposed to the whole peak oil thing. I wrote quite a bit about the prospect of places like Atlanta and Las Vegas not being able to function. It became self-evident that these were tremendous problems. After that book came out I was dwelling more and more on the petroleum story and it seemed to me that it deserved a book.

In *The Long Emergency*, which was the result of that, the oil story and its implications for daily life in America is in the foreground. Then, in the train behind that thought, comes the issue of the way our life depends on this increasingly scarce resource, including suburbia. I had written about suburbia in detail and described its shortcomings, and now

we're going to have to contend with the fact that it will fail.

So it's been a long haul for me with this issue. It is weird, to me, how the journey that I took from writing about the suburbs led me to writing about what is starting to be a comprehensive collapse of life as we've enjoyed it. I don't think this is the end of the world. I don't think life is over. I don't think American culture is over. But I do think that we are going to be living it very differently in the years ahead.

World Made By Hand

DC: After *The Long Emergency* you returned to fiction to explore how Americans might be living very differently in the not-so-distant future.

JHK: I did write a post-oil novel, called *World Made by Hand*, that was published in the spring of 2008, and a sequel called *The Witch of Hebron* in

2010. So I'm trying to take another look at the post-oil American future. But I also have a contract to write another nonfiction book about the diminishing returns of technology. That's something that I think is one of the great underappreciated elements of the story of our time: how we are screwing ourselves with our grandiose over-investments in complexity and ignoring the blow-back from them.

This whole energy story has never been about running out of oil, really.

It's about the breakdown of the complex systems that we depend on for the activity of everyday life. Because we've reached such an elaborate state of complexity and relative luxury in our living standard, we're going to be going through a difficult transition that will require us to de-complexify the systems that we depend on. And we'll probably experience something like lower living standards, although it doesn't necessarily mean that the quality of our life has to be worse.

Keep the Car Running?

Duncan Crary: In *The Long Emergency*, you go through a lot of the alternative fuel projects out there to keep the cars running. And you dismiss them all, for one reason or another.

James Howard Kunstler: Unfortu-nately there's a tremendous body of fantasy that has now grown among the American public about how we're going to keep on running our cars at all costs by other means than gasoline. Virtually all of these things are fantasies. You can do them as science projects on a small scale, but they don't scale up to two hundred million vehicles. You can run X number of vehicles on ethanol, or biodiesel, or French-fried potato oil that's been used and thrown out, but can you run the entire US automobile fleet, and the interstate highway system, and Walmart and Walt Disney World? Forget it. It ain't going to happen. All these alternative fuels, as far as liquid fuels for cars go—they're all net energy losers. I don't want to be misunderstood. I'm not against

---

In the Not-Distant Future...

DC: There's something I've noticed about these apocalypse movies like Mad Max. Do you notice that even in *Mad Max* they're all still driving cars?

JHK: Absolutely! One of the queerest things about that is that people are always imagining that my version of the future is like *Mad Max*, which couldn't be more wrong. *Mad Max* is a car chase.

DC: Even in Kevin Costner's *Waterworld*—there's no land left on Earth but they're still driving Jet Skis.

JHK: It's hilarious. In *World Made By Hand*, there's really only one car in the whole book, and it's moving under rather peculiar, pathetic and tragic circumstances. And it's not on stage very long before it stops running.

—James Howard Kunstler and Duncan Crary, February 28, 2008
KunstlerCast #3: "World Made By Hand"

alternative energy. But we're going to be disappointed in what these things can do for us.

DC: What about these hydrogen fuel cell cars that Honda is already leasing in California?

JHK: I don't think the hydrogen car is ever going to *really* happen. Now, look: you can't stop the big car companies from producing these stunts and PR shows that they're putting on. But just because they can produce one—or maybe twenty—hydrogen cars doesn't mean that a system is going to be in place for us to run one hundred or two hundred million of them. So I think that people who have invested their wishes and hopes in the hydrogen car are going to be very disappointed.

DC: What do you say to the idea that you can't replace gasoline with one alternative fuel, but how about a cocktail of alternative fuels? Let's use many different types of alternative fuel.

JHK: It's an understandable wish that we would want to keep our happy motoring system going, because we have invested so much in it, and it's almost inconceivable to most Americans that we would have to do without it. But I think the truth of the matter is that the automobile and all of the things associated with it are going to be a diminishing presence in our lives, whether we like it or not.

This is a symptom of our even larger inability to have a coherent discussion about our problems in this country. As you go around the country, what you realize is the only thing that we're talking about is how we're going to run the cars by some other means than gasoline or diesel fuel. To me, this is tragic, because we have to talk about a lot of other things.

I gave a lecture at Rensselaer Polytechnic Institute, and one young student got up and was going on at some length about all the technological means for producing new transit systems and new elegant ways of getting people from point A to point B. My response was that the one thing that we're never talking about is walkable cities or walkable neighborhoods.

It doesn't require any heroic new technologies or new discoveries. In fact, it is, when all is said and done, absolutely the most pleasant way to live and to get around. Anybody who's spent more than an hour and a half in the center of Paris understands this—or for that matter, a dozen other European cities.

The Colbert Nation

Colbert: What oil dilemma? I go the gas station, I pay money, they put gas in my car. What's the dilemma?

Kunstler: You're probably one of these people who thinks that the world has a creamy nougat center of oil, but it doesn't.

Colbert: No. When you go past the crust of the Earth you get to the Land of the Lost where the Sleestaks live.

Kunstler: That's right, but the trouble is that they've eaten up all the oil.

—James Howard Kunstler and Stephen Colbert, May 1, 2008, The Colbert Report

The Foreseeable Future

Duncan Crary: I gotta ask you about the Y2K thing. It seems to surface a lot during discussions about your peak oil, Long Emergency ideas. Stephen Colbert got in a jab about it when you went on *The Colbert Report* and it's on your Wikipedia page so it's not going to go away. Do you regret making predictions about what would happen after Y2K?

James Howard Kunstler: I took Y2K seriously, largely because there were a lot of obviously intelligent people on the Internet who were taking it seriously. And there was a broad enough array of them to persuade me that this was something that should be taken seriously, that you shouldn't just dismiss it.

From what I understand, in the aftermath, we spent an enormous amount of money on IT during that period. A lot of it was actually responsible for the Internet boom in the 1999-2000 period, just before that sort of blew up.

But I didn't really predict that the world would collapse. What I said was that Y2K was something that seemed to be pretty dangerous, and that we ought to pay attention to this, because a lot of systems could get into trouble. I don't think I said more than that.

DC: You did say that Y2K would rock our world.[9]

JHK: I thought it would rock our world in the sense that water systems would break down, there would be serious banking problems—especially when you are living in an era where so much money is digital and doesn't really exist in any other form except as a pixel on a screen or a couple of digital numbers in a server.

So it seemed to me that, under those circumstances, that was pretty perilous. What happened was that we didn't encounter huge interruptions in daily life, and everything seemed to go pretty well. What many scoffers don't really take into account is the amount of work and investment that went into mitigating the problem.

Just because we didn't have problems in banking, or municipal services, or electric power, or water treatment doesn't mean that we weren't in danger of having problems in those crucial areas. I said what I said, and I have to be responsible for it. People will probably continue to twang on me about it, but I don't think it was a mistake to take it seriously.

DC: Do you think that in order to get people to take a problem seriously so that they can fix it you need to ramp up the rhetoric?

JHK: I'm not really running a campaign for people to fix things. I am more interested in describing a situation than prescribing. Societies will go where they wanna go. Sometimes people in those societies make poor choices. Under the stress of the economic dislocations of the 1930s, some European countries made some bad choices and decided to become fascists or authoritarians of one kind or another. And they ended up creating a lot of mischief for the world, and a lot of misery, and a lot of tragedy and cruelty.

We are entering a period of economic dislocation, and I hope that we can greet it like grown-ups and respond to it intelligently, and be kind to our fellow human beings, and not be cruel, and not make the tragic choices that other groups of people have made. But there is no guarantee of that.

DC: Jim, you've been predicting the downfall of suburbia for quite some time because it's an unsustainable way of living —

JHK: Yeah, but not as a kind of Godzilla-like process. I haven't said a three-hundred-foot tyrannosaur is going to come through Levittown and breathe on it and burn it all down.

DC: But people still use your previous track record with Y2K to discredit your views on peak oil. They think peak oil is your new Y2K and that after peak oil doesn't bring suburbia to its knees, then you'll find some new threat to it. But given what's happening around us, it's getting harder to ignore your general forecast for America. Even some of your short-term predictions that you make in your Annual Forecast on your blog are panning out.

JHK: Yeah, and some people accuse me of being like the broken clock that's correct twice a day. But as I said, most of the work that I've done in terms of writing books about stuff for the last fifteen years, since I started with *The Geography of Nowhere*, most of that stuff has been, more or less, describing reality, more than necessarily predicting it. I understand the danger of making specific predictions, but I think there are some things that you can probably see the broad outlines of.

I think you can see the broad outlines of a society that is not going to be preoccupied with driving. I don't really know whether it will be in eighteen months or eighteen years, or one hundred and eighty years. I am quite confident that we will be in a society at some point that will not be cluttered up with cars, that will not be about driving.

Is the Long Emergency a Peak Oil Conspiracy Theory?

DC: One of the things that you say often is that you are allergic to conspiracy theories. But you also believe that President Obama and other authority figures are lying to us about our energy predicament. And that they've been lying to us for a long time...which kind of sounds like a conspiracy. Why are your ideas about peak oil *not* a conspiracy theory?

JHK: I guess you could say it's a *quasi* conspiracy. I do think that Mr. Obama is probably lying about our energy predicament, or at least the finer points of it.

The people who work with the US government and the people who are involved with American banking have their various interests and reasons for doing what they do. And I do believe that a lot of what they

do is to manipulate and mislead the American public—not for sinister reasons, but because they're desperate and they don't know what else to do.

They're afraid that if they actually reported reality to the American public that it would disrupt the economy and in particular the financial markets. The interplay between the government and the financial markets now is so complex and fragile that I think our oil situation has the capacity to get out of our control enough to make the unemployment rise much further than it is now and really drive down the American standard of living.

So it's perhaps a soft conspiracy—one that's not malign, although you could say that having good intentions isn't enough. It's not enough to just want America to be OK. By propping up longstanding deceitful practices that are getting you into more and more trouble you eventually risk actually collapsing your society because you've made so many bad choices.

DC: Even beyond the energy issues, it seems like there's a soft conspiracy in propping up suburbia as well. The government is lying to us that we can keep this system going through bailouts and banking tricks and alternative energy sources.

JHK: Yes, but I'm quite convinced that the consensus of the American public cannot imagine any other disposition of things except suburbia because that's what we've invested all of our wealth in. It's not like people are going to just pack up their stuff and put a padlock on the garage and leave their homes in suburban Schaumburg, Illinois, or suburban Milwaukee, or any other suburban place. We're kind of stuck with the infrastructure that we have at huge cost plopped there on the landscape.

DC: So you're saying that the psychology of previous investment is creating some kind of mass delusion about the health of suburbia?

JHK: It's simply a consensus—it's an agreement among a critical mass of individuals that something must be a certain way and that the story must be told a certain way. For us, the consensus is that we are a suburban nation and we can't imagine letting go of it. And we're not going to. We're going to prop it up at all costs.

So if that's a conspiracy, it's more like a conspiracy between leadership and the public to mutually lie and accept each other's lies and put out a narrative that people can live with. It's a strange kind of dependency-enabling relationship between the American public and their habits and the leadership which enables them to continue thinking that it's OK to keep on doing that.

But when large numbers of people start to accept a different story, and when leadership continues to tell the old story, that's when you get cognitive dissonance and political uproars and revolutions and disorders.

Doomers

Duncan Crary: Jim, a lot of people call you a "Doomer" because of your "Long Emergency" predictions. How do you feel about being called a "Doomer?"

James Howard Kunstler: I don't like the term applied to me because I don't consider myself a Doomer.[10] I consider myself to be a fairly cheerful guy with a certain point of view about where we're heading. But I'm not an Apocalyptarian. I just think that our way of life is a limited experience that is going to be changing. I don't consider that doom.

I think the accusation comes from a fear that these familiar comforts and ceremonies that we've enjoyed from the final blowout of the industrial experience and the final fiesta of cheap oil—people regard the loss of these things as a catastrophe, a collapse, as Armageddon. Human life can't possibly go on without Cheez Doodles, cable TV and SUVs. I sort of understand where they're coming from, and have a certain sympathy for it. But it's not my point of view.

DC: Some people use the Doomer label as a pejorative. But there are also people who wear the badge proudly. There are people who are into doom and gloom, right? On peak oil websites, even on your blog, you find people with screen names like "Dr. Doom."

JHK: Yes. Just as there are people who are cheerleading for the consumer economy to get back on its feet and continue, there is also a coterie of people who are cheerleading for the consumer economy to fall on its ass and for us to get away from it.

I put myself in that group. I would like to see the consumer economy discontinued as we've known it. It doesn't mean I don't want people to buy things again. But we obviously got this thing going at a level that was so destructive that it can't possibly continue without us destroying the Earth, destroying all the other beings that we share it with. Destroying, perhaps, even life itself. Who could

---

Doom and Gloom

Kunstler, in his book *The Long Emergency*, skips the evidence and the policy and decides that the end times are upon us…he takes clear glee in imagining the punishments Americans will endure for their profligate ways…His gloom is almost religiously deterministic; Americans have squandered their opportunities to repent. They have continued to drive and suburbanize. So now it is too late. Now is simply the time to suffer.

—Michael Manville, July 6, 2005
"Bomb The Suburbs: Bleatings of a reactionary environmentalist"*New York Press*

possibly want this to continue the way it has? So yes, I'm in favor of taking a different path.

I certainly enjoy a lot of the benefits of modern life. I wonder how we're going to get along without some of these things. But I'm prepared to go in that direction. I think we're going there anyway, whether we like it or not.

DC: I enjoy a good zombie flick, or apocalypse movie. And I wonder how many people are turning to the "Doomer" authors and websites just for entertainment, for what you call "Doomer porn." How can someone be taking this stuff seriously while they're clacking away on their keyboard posting comments to a blog all day?

JHK: Well everybody has a slightly different worldview and sense of where destiny is taking us. There is, I think, a general sense—which may be hardwired into our human sensibilities—that we like fresh starts. There's a certain appeal in wiping the slate clean. It comes up constantly in popular culture, even if it's just an interview with some pop star in *Vanity Fair* who says, "Oh yeah, I was a junkie then, but I went through rehab and now I'm a successfully high-functioning individual." Or someone who goes bankrupt and gets out from under their mountain of debt and is able to resume their life.

That's a big theme in human affairs from time immemorial. The more complex life has become for us, the more there is to sweep away, the more dross and the more junk that we need to clean out. So I think that that's a human wish, which is expressed at its most extreme in some of the Doomer sensibilities.

DC: Take a drive down the worst part of, say, Central Avenue in Albany,

New York, and look at all the crap there. The car dealerships, the strip malls. What would it take to get rid of that stuff? A meteor?

JHK: Exactly. You have the same sense when you go to Florida when you see all the crap on the landscape out there and you say, "Wow, it would really be great for a Category 5 hurricane to hit Vero Beach."

A Cleansing Spectacle

JHK: I have a vision from childhood, which persists in my memory, of being a nine-year-old boy in New York City and waiting for a big blizzard to hit. I remember the thrill of waiting for that storm to occur and then the joy of having the whole city just stand still for half a day after the storm had hit. It was just so wonderful for that silence to take over the huge bustle of Manhattan. For all the buses and the cars to stop. For the avenues to be free of cars and noise. For everything to just be still for a while.

I think there are many of us who don't necessarily get bummed out by an approaching storm. There's something wonderfully exciting about it. There's the idea that you're going to retreat into your shelter. You're going to view this interesting spectacle in safety and then you will emerge in a clean, fresh-smelling, rain-drenched, rain-cleansed world afterwards.

I think there's something in our human nature that very basically vibrates to these narratives and these patterns. There's obviously a condition in the world itself that we're very attuned to, of creation and destruction, life and birth, decline and death. We may affect to fight them, like, "I'm going to fight death. I'll live until I'm 130 years old. I'll follow this diet so that I'll never age and I'll be in great shape when I'm ninety-seven years old. I'll still be running marathons." But when all is said and done, everybody has to succumb to the overarching cycles of reality.

I think we all suspect that—even at the greatest scale—out of death comes rebirth. We're involved in a human system right now that's reached a point that many people probably think needs to die. I think it needs to die back some. I'd maybe give myself the pruning shears. I don't necessarily want to go and pull it out by the roots and toss it in the garbage heap of history. But I would like to prune it pretty severely.

From my point of view, my brand of Doomerism isn't about putting an end to human activity or the human race or civilization or a root canal or any of these things really. It's just about pruning out the plastic and the garbage. Letting the storm come and letting the rain come down. Cleaning out the system and going on.

Resurrection and redemption are great themes in the human story. I think we've got a few more cycles of it to go.

DC: Doesn't getting obsessed with the doom side of things also absolve us of some personal responsibility?

JHK: Yeah. I think you're quite right. That's one of the reasons that I don't even want to be grouped with people who say, "Well it's all hopeless. I give up. I don't care about the human race. I don't care about where we go from here. It's just all screwed up and hopeless. Forget about it." Because I don't feel that way. I'm very interested in the project of civilization and I'm interested in the good things that the human race has created. I would like these things to go forward.

Spreading the Word

DC: When you go around the country telling people this story of suburbia and "The Long Emergency," how do they react? Do they "get it?"

JHK: I go in front of all kinds of groups including some who really don't get it. I remember talking to the International Council of Shopping Center Developers. They really didn't get it. But they weren't obnoxious about it. They politely listened to what I had to say. When I finished talking to them, they just started chatting up all of their plans for building more parking structures, after I told them that car storage is probably not going to be the programming of the future. They didn't hear a darn thing.

DC: Does that upset you when that happens?

JHK: I guess I'm not overly concerned with how well they get it or whether they get it. I'm just doing my thing and if they get it, fine, and if they don't get it, then I just go onto the next bunch.

One thing I encounter is people saying "Give us solutions." Most of the people asking for solutions want to be able to behave exactly the way we're behaving now. All of this delusional thinking is preventing us from finding a way of life that we're going to be able to carry on.

DC: But do you ever offer advice to these people who ask you for "solutions?"

JHK: You bet. You know, the college audiences universally complain that they want hope. "Can't you give me some hope?" I am not a hope dispenser to passive consumers of hope. But I think I'm a very cheerful, upbeat person. I'm not necessarily a rosy-eyed optimist, but I'm a happy person and I believe that we're going to continue on. So what I tell them is that the main thing that distinguishes a successful adult from a child is that an adult knows the difference between wishing for stuff and making it happen.

There's a whole long list of intelligent things that we can respond to this set of circumstances with. We need to be out there actively fixing our civilization, reforming the way we do our farming, our commerce, our schooling and our trade. And building our cities and designing our homes and our buildings and all the things that are necessary to be part of a civilization. We're going to have to put a lot more thought and work into that.

As we do that, I'm serenely convinced that we will become a much more hopeful people. In fact, if anything, all the marvels and technological miracles of the past one hundred years have only ended up producing a society which is profoundly unhappy, depressed and anxiety-ridden. We really have nowhere to go but up from here.

DC: Do you think that if you had children, you'd have a different worldview about all that's going on here in America?

JHK: I suppose that I would. Most of the people I know have a kind of desperate feeling about their children, and so far as I don't have any, I don't have that kind of desperation.

DC: …because their kids are going to be around for this mess.

JHK: Yeah, I understand that. I'm not an idiot.

DC: I didn't mean to imply you were.

JHK: I know plenty of people who have children, and I see how they feel about them and act around them. It's human nature to want to feel that you're going to be OK. That you're going to occupy a safe place. That there's going to be some warm hearth for you somewhere and a warm and soft tranquil place to curl up and go to sleep. And that there will be people with you and you will hear music in the next room. These are all very human. But it doesn't mean we have to have Walmart to do that. We don't have to have two hundred and forty million cars to feel OK about being alive.

I'm confident that the human race is going to go forward. I just think that the human adventure goes through different story lines, and we've come to the end or nearly the end of one story line—the high-tech industrial fantasia. Now we're entering something else. I think it'll be just as exciting. We've just got to remember to wash our hands and stuff.

DC: You've said that "The journey from point A to B needs to be rewarding," and that "To entice people into the cities you need to reward them." In some ways, do you feel that our leaders need to reward and entice the people with some hope, because they're not going to motivate them by scaring them and depressing them?

JHK: I don't know. Winston Churchill got up in front of the British people and said, "All I can offer you right now is blood, sweat and tears," and they responded to that because they understood the urgency of the situation. He didn't get up and say, "You're going to have more salad shooters and marshmallows and ranch dressing next month." So again, we really need to stop being softheaded softies and harden up a little bit, and grow up a little bit.

T. Boone Pickens

T Boone Pickens: I don't know whether you've seen this guy…his last name's Kunstler and it's not the guy that was the lawyer back years ago…in the Chicago Seven.…I went over to SMU and heard him the other night. He is worth hearing. He is a generalist, but he tells us where we made the mistakes. We didn't develop our rail system.

You know, you look at the world today. We go places and we want to ride on a two-hundred-mile-an-hour train. We have to go to a foreign country to do that. We don't have that. Why don't we have it? Because they had cheap oil. It didn't make sense for us to. It was expensive. We were going to subsidize it and you know it just didn't make sense for us.

And…we built too far away from our work. He says you're going to…move to your work now because of the cost of energy. And it was really interesting because this was two years ago and the guy nailed it. I've listened to what he's had to say. I watched what's happened and he's right on.

—Billionaire Texas oilman T. Boone Pickens, July 22, 2008
*Testimony before the Senate Homeland Security
and Government Affairs Committee*

Retooling Suburbia

Duncan Crary: I want to hear your thoughts on retrofitting suburbia for a post-peak oil future. Or just a future with less driving. But we should probably begin by acknowledging that not all suburbs are created equal—they're not all just endless housing tracts. Some of the older ones have some sort of downtown areas that could be built up.

James Howard Kunstler: All suburbs are not identical. There are wide variations in the quality of them. In the East you have many suburbs that started as railroad suburbs with actual downtowns—places like Westport, Connecticut, or Larchmont, or Brookline, Massachussetts. As you go into the South and the West you get less of that, and the suburbs are just one mass of sprawling strip malls and collector boulevards. These are places of varying quality and they lend themselves to varying degrees for retrofit.

DC: But even in the worst plastic cul-de-sac in a typical suburban development—couldn't you still convert those houses into a grocery store, a carpenter's place, a hardware store?

The Future of New Urbanism

The future of New Urbanism is in urban villages and rural communities—in both. It's in the extremes. It's no longer in the in-between.

—Jaime Correa, May 28, 2009
KunstlerCast #67: "The 40 Percent Plan"
interview with Duncan Crary

JHK: You could, especially if you changed the zoning laws so that it was permitted. However, it raises a lot of troubling implications. Sure, you could put a corner store and a few other things in the middle of a giant subdivision of one thousand houses in California. But I really wonder whether the rest of that organism is going to work at all without the kind of cheap motoring that it was designed for in the first place. If you're in a subdivision of one thousand acres in California or Colorado or Georgia, and it's three-quarters of a mile to a little store at the center of the thing or at the edge of it, I'm not sure it's going to work for people.

The basic template among New Urbanists for a workable neighborhood or urban quarter is based on the idea of the quarter-mile walk. That's the radius of the size of what that neighborhood can be to work effectively for people, because people aren't comfortable venturing further than that. We have all these places in America that simply defy that formula. It's not even that I'm being so psychologically rigid, because I certainly can imagine that people would adapt to something if they really had to. But I'm not convinced that it's that workable. As I said in *The Long Emergency*, the Jolly Green Giant isn't going to come along and move all these houses closer together.[11] They are where they are.

DC: I get a decent number of emails from people who feel trapped in suburbia.

JHK: They're even more trapped now than they were a year or so ago because their situation has gotten worse. Not only is the value of their property going down, but now there's the whole question about whether they're going to have any job at all, or any income at all, or even be able to stay there.

Some of the more catastrophic places in America are simply being abandoned, like in Florida where the real estate market collapsed. So that's already begun in some parts of the country and we may see it creeping from the margins to the more normal places, whether it's the suburbs outside Minneapolis, Dayton, Dallas or wherever. I personally believe that the majority of these suburban places won't make it, at least not in the optimum way that we wish they would—by being retrofitted. That's partially because we're going to be less affluent, but it's also because I think that our populations, after a certain point, are going to start declining, not increasing.

We're not going to see any more expansion or growth of things. We're going to be seeing a generalized contraction and shrinking back of stuff. The stuff that doesn't work very well will not necessarily be retrofitted or rebuilt, it will simply be abandoned for a while.

Suburban Ghettos of the Future

DC: You believe that the suburbs of today will become the ghettos of the future.

JHK: I think that suburbs as a general proposition are going to become devalued. In the natural course of things, the old real estate—the stuff getting beat up—becomes the cheap real estate. That's why the poor people tend to gravitate toward it.

There's something else about retooling suburbia, and that has to do with the question of, "Will Americans be able to grow any significant amount of food in suburban places?" By sprawling out all over the landscape, we've destroyed some of the best agricultural land close to the old cities. That land is no longer available. Instead, the way we grow food in the United States, for the most part, is in huge monocultures of corn and wheat—produced by way of huge petroleum and fossil fuel inputs and diesel fuel to move it around and plow the soil and move the products three thousand miles, etc. That's our system of producing food. And it's about to get into a lot of trouble because the money's just not there to fork over for the fertilizers, the herbicides, the diesel fuel and all the things that you need to get up and running every April.

Chapter 3: American Culture

———————— Social Critic ————————

Duncan Crary: You're better known as a commentator than as a novelist.

James Howard Kunstler: And the publishers will tell you that nonfiction just sells better than fiction does. Fewer people read novels nowadays. That's just the way it is—it's not the nineteenth century anymore.

DC: Would you rather be writing fiction, creating art?

JHK: I *would* rather be writing fiction. I'd rather be writing the next two installments of *World Made By Hand*, which I fully intend to get to.

However, I just like composing prose and I like doing it in nonfiction as well as fiction. I get a bang out of it. And I'm very fortunate that I can choose my own subject matter.

I think what a lot of people don't quite get about me is that my writing is much more about prose artistry than it is about dredging up facts about the petroleum industry or politics or resource issues. I'm much more interested in exercising my skills—particularly my malicious sense of humor. My books are as much about comedy as they are about the subject matter. *The Long Emergency*, as dire as it was, was very consciously crafted to be full of gags—because, as I said in one of my earlier books, it's the unfortunate fate of the ridiculous to be ridiculed.[1]

We have become a ridiculous nation lurching around through an impossible situation. It's close to a Charlie Chaplin movie. We're literally becoming a slapstick clown nation, if we weren't before. Perhaps we were just as bad in 1932, I don't know.

"The American Way of Life is Not Negotiable."

This was the basic mental algorithm for the United States in the first eight years of the twenty-first century, the idea that the American way of life is non-negotiable.

One thing the American public doesn't realize is that when you don't negotiate the circumstances that the universe sends your way, you get assigned a new negotiating partner called Reality. And then it negotiates for you. You don't even have to be in the room. You can go watch Internet porn, or play poker online, or eat Cheez Doodles and drink Pepsi, or watch NASCAR. And then your life will be negotiated for you.

— James Howard Kunstler, February 10, 2010
lecture hosted by the Stakeholders,
at Sage College, Albany, New York

Mencken, Wolfe and Beckett

DC: H.L. Mencken was a writer from that era who was commenting on the ridiculousness of America at the time. You and he are similar in ways. You have your "NASCAR morons" and he had his "Boobus Americanus."

JHK: I was influenced by Mencken when I was a kid. I remember the first book of his that I just stumbled on—a collection of his essays. That was the summer of 1967. It was a really galvanizing moment, being eighteen years old and being exposed to that extremely muscular comic prose. He really had it down and he really had a style that was his.

Mencken was a journalist who is almost completely forgotten, whose heyday was from 1910 to about 1945, when he kind of faded away. He was especially popular during the 1920s, which was a wild era of excess in the USA and it was a great kind of circus for him to observe. One of the greatest acts in the many rings of the American circus back then was "The Scopes Monkey Trial," which he famously covered in Tennessee, where they tried to convict a biology teacher for teaching evolution. Mencken went down there and savagely covered the proceedings. The attorney recruited to prosecute this biology teacher named John Scopes was a former presidential candidate, William Jennings Bryan, who had run as a Democrat at the turn of the century and lost three times. Bryan was a religious nut. He was sick and seedy and his hair was falling out in patches and he looked weird dressed in weird antique Midwest costumes that were kind of laughable to big-city people. So Mencken took great delight in mocking him. He had a malicious sense of humor, too.

The cherry on top of the whole thing was that poor William Jennings Bryan died five days after the trial ended. Mencken wrote a vicious obituary. It was one of the more vicious things ever published in American journalism—but also very funny. That was pretty much his high spot.

The twenties came and went, and the standard view of Mencken was that he wasn't really able to adjust his views to the realities of the Depression and the hardship that people were suffering—his humor didn't go over very well as that went on. He was also fairly pro-German because he was proud of his German ancestry. He had carried on quite a bit during the First World War about the acts that had been legislated against the German-Americans at that time, 1917-18. So when the Second World War rolled around he was considered to be an unappetizingly pro-German character, and the public sentiment really started going against him. He sort of faded away. Then in 1948 he had a massive stroke. He lived on another seven years, and passed away unnoticed in Baltimore in 1956.

DC: Do you find yourself using any of his techniques in your own commentary?

JHK: I have consciously done everything I can to *not* copy the way he expressed himself. I use the em dashes a lot. But otherwise I'm trying to avoid anything that smacks of him.

DC: Are there any other critics out there or writers who have influenced your style?

JHK: I had a similar galvanizing moment when Tom Wolfe exploded on the pages of the *Herald Tribune* Sunday supplement back in 1963. I was just getting to the point of being a young adult, fourteen–fifteen years old, and reading a lot. Growing up in New York City, I was exposed to a lot of high and low culture of exactly the kind that he was covering. So I was familiar with some of it.

His prose was spectacular. He was able to put it across funny and also make a point. That was before I encountered Mencken by maybe three, four years. I discovered with these two guys, Mencken and Tom Wolfe, that I wanted to write comic discursive prose about issues that were important and interesting. It was still a little bit hard for me to sort out the issues, though—I mean I wasn't sitting down and writing essays about American culture.

I spent my college years being a theater major, so I got sidetracked from my interest in literature, although it ended up helping because one of the big influences on me was Samuel Beckett. Beckett was an Irish playwright who ended his days with the twentieth century. He was very prominent and popular in the late sixties, his best-known play being *Waiting for Godot*, which people make reference to still. I was in that play and toured in it quite a bit. We got some kind of grant from the state of New York to take it all over. So I was on the road with this play living like a vaudevillian at the age of nineteen.

Waiting for Godot is an absurdist 1960s abstract piece, but it's full of wonderfully written dialogue and truly beautifully composed images— Beckett was a wonderfully lyrical writer. One of the things it taught me was that it was possible to incorporate lyricism with comic writing. I became interested in that. So by the time I graduated from college and dumped my theater career and got into the newspaper game, I was interested in writing stuff that was comical and lyrical about things that matter. Eventually, I became a social critic in the mold of what Mencken had been doing in the twenties, but I'm living in a very different world.

Managing the Critic Persona

DC: Do you separate your critic persona from the person you are when you're not wearing your critic's hat—Jim Kunstler, the guy who lives in Saratoga and shops in the grocery store?

JHK: I don't know if it's psychologically healthy or not but my persona does feel compartmentalized, although it's not difficult for me to go in and out of the different personas that I'm familiar with. The guy who goes downtown to the supermarket and meets his friends is very different from the guy who sits in front of a video display, pushing pixels around, making sentences and think-ing about what's going on politically and economically in the country. This has to do with the fact that my personality is largely that of a comedian. When all is said and done, I'd rather be funny and crack jokes than be serious. It takes effort for me to be serious and my way of being serious often involves me trying to be funny.

DC: But the people who know you through your public critic persona—some of them are disappointed or maybe even looking to attack you if they see you driving your pickup truck or flying around. So how do you deal with that? How do you react to the criticisms of the critic?

JHK: I've been kind of a low-rent public figure. I put stuff out there—

DC: You put stuff out there that hits certain nerves, so people want to see: where does this guy live? What does this guy drive? What does this guy eat?

JHK: I think that the public is almost always disappointed when they run into a public figure of some kind, whether it's Brat Pitt or me. They're always disappointed to discover that you're wearing a certain kind of sneaker or that you're driving a pickup truck or that you're flying three thousand miles to Seattle.

DC: Do you feel any obligation to live up to the expectations of Kunstler, the critic?

JHK: I feel an obligation to be a decent human being. I feel an obligation to pay attention to people who are asking for it under reasonable terms. I answer all my email, even from cranks. Even if it's only a two-sentence response.

DC: Or two words: Fuck you.

JHK: I very rarely say that—usually only when someone writes to me calling me a Jew bastard faggot moron or something. Once in a while I am in a bad mood or they catch me at the wrong time and I'll say something mean back.

Pass the Cheez Doodles

DC: So what do you say when someone finds you at the strip mall in suburbia buying a bag of Cheez Doodles and hopping in your car?

JHK: I don't feel hypersensitive about it. I'm perfectly comfortable with the idea that I'm a creature of my time and place. We all do tend to be hostages to our time and our place and the manner and modes of our time and place. So I'm not embarrassed about that at all. I bought a bag of Cheez Doodles the other night to go to a little cocktail reception for a friend who was starting a new job. I just felt like, it's never a party unless the Cheez Doodles are there. So I got me a bag, and you know what? I ate a few of them. Hardly anyone else would touch them because they seem to be radioactive, but I had a few.

DC: Every year I go to your holiday party and there's usually a bowl of Cheez Doodles or something like that. At this recent one you had a bowl of Cheez Doodles.

JHK: I always have 'em. You just don't really sniff 'em out. They're there.

DC: This year, people were standing around them thinking, "Oh, he's being ironic." And I was thinking, "I think he's just putting out a bowl of Cheez Doodles."

JHK: Yeah!

DC: I don't know that you're deliberately being ironic, are you?

JHK: No. I don't even like the ironic stance that has been so popular in my generation. You can't really develop that overall ironic stance about life unless everything in your life is fucking ridiculous. There is a lot about American life that is ridicu-

lous. But I refuse to submit to being a victim of the ridiculousness of it. So I'm not going to just stand by and say, "Oh, isn't all our ridiculous shit cute?" That's why I'm not into kitsch. Because I believe if something was really stupid and shitty the first time, you shouldn't bring it back and celebrate it for its shittyness. So I don't do that. It doesn't do anything for me.

DC: How has being a social critic affected your personal relations? Do you find your friends are getting upset with you sometimes with the things you're saying about America or the suburbs?

JHK: My close friends where I live have very little connection with my writing life. They're not necessarily reading everything I write. They're people who think that my Long Emergency ideas are crazy. Some of them think that I'm nuts thinking that there's some kind of a problem out there with America. Now I don't necessarily hang out with the kind of suburban people that you'd find in one of these boom cities of the last fifty years. I don't live in Dallas or Orlando or Phoenix. If I lived in a place like that, I'd probably encounter people who are more defensive or angry about a viewpoint that opposes what they've invested in. But I'm not. I know very few people who live in anything that I would remotely call standard-issue suburbia. I have very few friends who are violently defending anything that I'm yapping about.

DC: —about suburbia. But they think the Long Emergency energy issues are a little whacky?

JHK: They're not necessarily paying attention. They're not familiar with Jeff Brown's Export Land Theory. They don't look at the EIA figures.[2] They're not paying attention to TheOilDrum.com. They're really just going about their lives. And the supermarket's still full of stuff. And despite all of the disarray in the financial sector, they're still getting paid. I don't know many people who have been tossed out of their job.

— Throwaway Culture and the Plastic Fantastic —

Duncan Crary: I think a lot about our sense of entitlement to convenience in America. Take all the throwaway plastic bags and plastic spoons out there—we are a people who are so lazy and entitled that we can't be bothered wiping off a metal spoon and saving it for tomorrow. We create utensils for one-time use. And now the spoon that you ate one plastic cup of yogurt with, and the plastic bag they came in, are all going to be around for eternity in some landfill.

James Howard Kunstler: That's how extravagant the plastic fiesta was. You get a certain period of history, a brief hundred-year period, where you throw a party, and it's been a big party. It's largely a petroleum party, a cheap oil party. And it created a lot of trash. So what we're seeing is the trash that's being thrown out from the party we threw for ourselves.

DC: You often refer to "Our throwaway culture" in America.

Redundant Acquisition

We're leaving a time in our economy when a huge amount of making money was concerned with getting people to redundantly acquire the same machine so that everybody had to have their own lawnmower and laundry machine on the premises. It is nice to be able to wash something instantly when you need it, but that's the kind of thing you can work around—you discover that you can systematize the way you do laundry if you plan ahead. And it's the same thing with transportation, you can plan ahead to get to a place if you don't have your own car if your culture is intelligent enough to design systems that allow you to do that.

—James Howard Kunstler, June 16, 2011
KunstlerCast #160 "Housing Bubble Update"

JHK: It's one of the appalling features of our life, and for me it's not just the plastic spoons and the old sneakers and the faded broken Barbie dolls—

DC: —and the inflatable alligators—

JHK: —and the Frosty the Snowman Christmas ornaments and all that crap. For me it's much more a matter of the buildings that we built, and the things that have really become the hardscape of our everyday world.

That concerns me, largely because it's so depressing. It damages our spirits so badly, and this is apart from whatever the plastic is doing to our mitochondria or whatever diseases that it's causing. Just the daily surroundings of all these terrible crappy buildings, and all the signage, and all the crap connected to automobiling, has a tremendously corrosive effect on our spirit.

—— Americans Are Scary-Looking and Infantile ——

Duncan Crary: There are an awful lot of tattooed Americans out there these days, which is something you're not happy about. What's your beef with tattoos?

James Howard Kunstler: Tattoos, historically, have been the calling cards of cannibals, whores and sailors. This is activity that belongs in the margins, not on Main Street. So it's disappointing to see the mainstreaming of tattoos, today.

DC: Was there a particular moment or incident that set you off?

JHK: I started to develop a bad attitude about tattoos when I started going to a particular gym in town—there are all these muscleheads there who are covered with tattoos and there are more and more of them every week, including many females.

Some of the tattoos I'm seeing these days are just so alarming. There are guys who have flames tattooed up their necks. I saw one kid on the street in front of the tattoo parlor on our main drag and he had a dotted line tattooed on his neck with a pair of scissors tattooed on one end and the words "Cut Here" tattooed on the other end. It was just sickening to see that a young man had such a desperate and depraved view of his own value that he was advertising for someone to cut his head off. It was appalling. I think this is an attempt for the marginal to invade the center and I am all for keeping the marginal on the margins.

DC: One of your observations is that Americans are scary-looking.

We look like fierce warriors with all these tattoos.

JHK: I think we are trying to make ourselves scary-looking. What it tells me is that we are a very insecure people right now. We've got to make ourselves look like characters out of a *Road Warrior* movie or make ourselves look like some kind of barbarian culture in order to feel secure and OK about ourselves.

DC: Why?

JHK: We have a lot of reasons to be insecure. It's very hard for young people especially to imagine some kind of a plausible career for themselves. There are a lot of things that have been foreclosed to them. There is very little possibility of many of them ever finding blue-collar work that will pay them a decent wage. There are very few jobs that are appealing to a young man. You think

On the Death of Michael Jackson

I don't want to be cruel about it, because he was a pathetic man—he had feelings like everybody else, and wishes, and things that he loved, I'm sure. But he did represent a lot of weird things about us, especially our tendency to lie to ourselves about who we are, what's happening and what we're doing.

I did notice over the last couple of weeks that whenever they showed a picture of him in the media, it was always one of these pictures from about 1982, before he put himself through this really monstrous transformation that made him look like a character from another planet or from a horror movie or something. That's the way that people want to remember him.

But it's just amazing how much we're sweeping under the rug, just as we sweep all these things about our current predicament as a nation under the rug—the damage we've done to our culture and the bad choices that we've made.

To me, Michael Jackson represents a lot of the bad choices that America made about itself and its difficulty in telling the truth about it.

—James Howard Kunstler, July 16, 2009
KunstlerCast Grunt: "Jacko"

a young man wants to be a Walmart associate? Right now, young men are being foreclosed out of any kind of meaningful role in their society. And I think this insecurity is being broadcast now in the way they are presenting themselves to the public.

Hip-Hop Costuming and the Infantilization of Men

JHK: It's not just the tattoos. Another thing that fascinates me is the costuming—the costuming that has come out of hip-hop, for example, which features oversized shirts and pants that make you look like your legs are very short. What this tells me is that American men feel like babies and they want to portray themselves like babies. Babies have very large torsos and short legs. So American young men are dressing up in costumes that make them look like babies and then you add a sideways hat and sneakers that aren't tied and you really look like an infant.

DC: I've seen grown men dressed like that—with an oversized polo shirt. And yeah, I thought it was a kid until he turned around and it was actually a 45-year-old man.

JHK: The infantilization of young men in our culture is becoming really striking.

DC: I've never heard anyone approach the topic that way. I have heard that the droopy jeans come from prison culture.

JHK: I think they did originally. Then they circulated through the ghetto for about twenty years. But in the ghetto you have a situation where you have children who are being raised in households where men are not present. Why are they not present? Partly because a lot of the fathers are in prison. So you have men who are in prison, you don't have male role models and you have male children being raised by mothers. And those men dress up in costumes that make them look like babies.

Eventually it led to some very strange cultural manifestations. Especially as that programming moves through the whole broad culture, not just the black community but out into the white former working-class community, where they are suffering terribly from lost incomes and not having any plausible idea of what to do with themselves—what kind of vocations to go into.

Warrior Culture

DC: And you also believe there is a warrior culture message being added to the mix through the "gangsta" rap, which is not just in the ghettos but is being massively consumed by white suburban teenagers, of course.

JHK: I have maintained for the last fifteen years that what became mainstream hip-hop was really a warrior culture. But notice that it's being masked and concealed behind a uniform of baby clothes…so that it looks like it's harmless. But in fact, it is a warrior culture.

Let me clarify something. Young men tend to gravitate to warrior cultures. I think we are hardwired for that as human beings who have only recently emerged from the hunter-gatherer stage of development. So we are really hardwired to be warriors as males, and yet you have a whole generation of warriors who are not being trained to be warriors. They are being trained to be babies—to be helpless, to not know how to do things, to be illiterate, to be not conversant with their own history. That has an effect on your destiny.

DC: It seems like you stirred up the hornets with this topic after you wrote about it on your website.[3] There's been quite a reaction online.

JHK: What interests me is the indignation that my attitude provokes from the tattooed people and the people wearing the hip-hop clothes—that whole cohort of young people. It's as though they are saying, "We have a right to present ourselves this way. We like presenting ourselves this way and it makes sense to us to present ourselves this way. So don't get down on us for doing it because we have every right to do it and we feel good doing it this way."

What I would have to say in response to that is, "Yeah, if you are facing a very uncertain destiny, and you are very insecure, and your society is not giving you much to feel hopeful about, and your society is not preparing you for the kind of life that you are going to be facing in your later decades—then sure, present yourself as a violent clown." Because that is what young men in America look like now: violent clowns.

DC: I don't have one, but I know a lot of people with tattoos. Everybody seems to have one. To me, tattoos are just another empty gesture in America. People are just broadcasting their "individuality"—externally—in lock step with what's hip and cool today.

JHK: Sure. It's like saying, "I'm a nonconformist, just like you."

DC: It does seem like the "emos" and the "goth" people and even the bikers all shop at the same store. All the emos go the emo store. All the bikers go the Harley-Davidson store. And they purchase their outfits that all look the same.

JHK: They're all just bullshit consumer cultures of one kind or another. Tattoos are just another kind of consumer item. It's just a service that you pay for. It doesn't make you a better person. It doesn't make you someone with more knowledge. It doesn't make you more heroic. It just makes you someone who went and spent $150 on a picture that's on your skin.

DC: Does anything else bother you about tattoos?

JHK: There's an interesting element of it that we see in other areas of life. Having become such a television-ized culture and people, what you see is an impulse to put a picture on everything. You use yourself as a television to broadcast stories about yourself saying, "I'm a lover," "I'm a fighter," "I'm a valiant warrior."

DC: Or "I'm a sojer"…but they've never been in the army before.

JHK: To some extent, I can accept that a tattoo can just be another kind of ornament. I think that within limits there is nothing wrong with that. It's just that when you turn yourself into a grotesque billboard and you start projecting messages like "Kill me now" or "I hate you" or "I'm a vicious thug," that ends up being socially unhelpful.

Dude, We've Got Technology

Duncan Crary: Something you try to impart on your audience is, "You can't put technology into a gas tank." People don't always realize that—that you need juice to run the gizmos. You caught that attitude firsthand at the Google offices. What happened?

James Howard Kunstler: I was invited to give a talk at the Google headquarters in the Silicon Valley a few years ago. It was really a typical jive plastic office park building in a wasteland of off-ramps and free parking and all the other crap that

California is so famous for and that has spread everywhere else in America.

The building itself was tricked out like a kindergarten inside. They had foosball games and ping-pong tables and Nok Hockey and Lucite boxes full of gummy bears and yogurt-covered pretzels. And you could see where they were coming from—there had been this whole idea in corporate enterprise in America for a while that the more childlike you are, that means you're more creative. So there's a great striving out there now to be as childlike as possible.

The executives and senior engineers were all dressed like skateboard rats—they're wearing sideways hats, their ass crack was showing because they're wearing pants that are falling down…because they're being creative and childlike and playful.

Jiminy Cricket Syndrome

Probably the biggest impediment to our thinking is what I call the Jiminy Cricket Syndrome. This is the belief that's now become normal for all Americans, that when you wish upon a star, your dream comes true. This used to be a normal belief for seven-year-olds in America. It's now become a normal belief for everyone in America. And it's a dangerous idea.

—James Howard Kunstler, February 10, 2010
lecture hosted by the Stakeholders,
at Sage College, Albany, New York

So I went into the auditorium and gave a talk about oil. At the end we had questions. There were no questions, there was only one comment that was repeated seventeen times: "Like, dude, we've got technology." Subtext: "You're an asshole, we've got technology."

It's scary that at the highest level of American corporate high-tech enterprise, they don't know the difference between technology and energy. Do you know how fundamental that is, and how dangerous that is, to not understand the difference between these things? Most Americans don't understand that technology and energy are different—that they're not interchangeable. That if you run out of one, you just can't swap it out with the other one. You can't just plug in technology where you were once using energy. This is one of the great delusions of our time. And

it's coming from Google! That tells you something. If they can't think straight about that, what about the people at the ball bearing factory or the people who make bowling trophies?

The general psychology of America these days is that some mythological mad scientist "they" will come up with some miracle rescue remedy to get us out of this problem. It's not likely to happen.

The Virtual is Not an Adequate Replacement for the Authentic

DC: Something in the back of my mind, as we talk about sprawl and the built environment, is that there's a whole other public sphere we inhabit in this modern life—the virtual realm. The Internet has become a public space of sorts, and I wonder what effect that has had on the public spaces in our tangible world.

JHK: It's been a very interesting and in some ways magical adventure that we've taken ourselves on. Like anything in the human experience, it's going to have repercussions and unintended consequences and diminishing returns. I think we can begin to see them start to resolve pretty clearly now. One thing is of course that there is probably nothing that destroys time in your life more than the Internet.

The one thing that the Internet doesn't do is give you more hours in the day. In fact it gobbles them up like Pac-Man so that we all become hostages—if not to the alternative universe of stuff out there, to some of the routine functions of it, like email and messaging and stuff that you just can't get away from.

DC: I used to work in a newsroom almost ten years ago now where there was one computer with the Internet. We used to complain about how inefficient that was and how much better it would be if we all had Internet at our desktops. Now that everyone does, I feel like it's not more efficient after all. It was more efficient to only have fifteen minutes to look something up online.

JHK: Right, because now everybody is spending three-quarters of their time looking at Internet porn, or doing video poker, or reading interesting things on Wikipedia, or emailing their grandmother. It tells us a lot about why we're having such a hard time even constructing a broad-based social agreement about what reality is about these days. We're in desperate need of attending to reality, and yet by some happenstance we've created the world's most amazing distraction from reality that has ever been invented. We've created a way for the entire population of the

USA to not pay attention to what's going on in our culture, and in our economy, and our society. It explains a lot about how paralyzed we are and how unable we are to form any kind of plan of action for what we're going to do. You've got a whole nation now that's mentally masturbating for huge amounts of time every day.

DC: How do you think this emphasis on the virtual realm affects the tangible realm?

JHK: What it's doing is impoverishing us. The virtual is not an adequate replacement for the authentic. As much as we may like it or find it appealing or find it ingenious, it's just not good enough. And we've got to stop kidding ourselves that virtual life is as good as real life.

DC: I don't want to sound hypocritical—I'm on the Internet all the time—but the Internet is just one more thing that is eroding a sense of place.

JHK: Although the sense of place in the USA was pretty damaged well before the Internet came along. In fact it may actually be that because we were already in that situation, the Internet became all that more appealing—because the public realm in America had been destroyed, and it became nothing more than this universal automobile slum.

Then all of a sudden the Internet comes along, and here's a landscape of the mind that will take you anywhere, and you can spend endless amounts of time exploring it. The one thing about human cognition, the human mind, though, is I think that we are hardwired for exploring. This is a very important characteristic of the human mentality—we're natural explorers, and when presented with interesting opportunities for exploration, we will tend to take them. Even if they happen at the expense of real life, which is what's happening to us with the Internet.

The Third Place

DC: Has the Internet become our Third Place?[4]

JHK: For sure.... Even in my town, which is pretty high caliber—with some educated people and a small college in it—there really is no watering hole that I would go to at five o'clock in the afternoon to meet kindred spirits to sit around and talk. There's nothing like a pub where I could reliably go to find people who I could have some meaningful social exchange with.

That really needs to occur in an organic way. You need to have those five or six people actually show up in a geographic location or it just doesn't work. So in my world, unless you make a concerted effort to invite six of your friends over for dinner or something, you will never see them. You'll never see these other people except by accident on the street.

DC: I'm fortunate in my little city where I can just go out and meet those five people. Not the same five people, but there are always a reliable number of folks out that I know and enjoy being with.

JHK: Do you have a hangout bar?

DC: Sure. We bounce around, but there's one bar in particular called Ryan's Wake where we tend to meet up regularly at around five p.m. It's right on the river, by the drawbridge.

My friends who are my age don't understand how I can have a social life without a cell phone and texting—because I don't have those things. But I can always find a friend out and about in town and it feels more natural and exciting that way. That seems so old-fashioned and archaic to my peers.

JHK: It's funny. I see you frequently, but never drunk on your ass. Is that a condition that I don't know about that you're mostly in or something?

DC: That's my third place, the pub. It's an old-fashioned kind of arrangement.

JHK: Both of us are guys who work on our own, where we have solitary workspaces. I don't know about you, but I go through whole workdays where I don't really talk to other people or meet them in the flesh. In spite of the fact that I'm getting a lot of electronic communications, I get hungry to see real people in real situations. I don't hang around bars, really. I don't even hang around the coffee shop that much, although I kind of like to go there. But I get hungry for human society, and it's a little hard for me to get to.

DC: I get hungry for that human interaction, too. But I'm very fortunate that I can walk out my front door and get it. That's what I really love about working and living in a business district. I'm surrounded by other little shops and offices and friends. And I can make little trips around the neighborhood to visit my accountant, or buy office supplies, or check in on a client, or grab lunch. I actually look forward to doing my chores because of that.

Chapter 4: Architecture

The Starchitects

Duncan Crary: What's the story behind these scary techno-futuristic buildings in just about every big city? Like the Seattle Central Library, what's up with that building? It looks like a droid transport carrier from a George Lucas flick except it's made of glass. It also looks like it's about to fall over.

James Howard Kunstler: It's not that hard to understand what's going on. The city officials are…not that sophisticated. They're probably not stupid, but what they're hoodwinked into is a status fashion contest with other cities. And the big status symbol for the last twenty years has been to get a museum or a library designed by one of a certain roster of star architects or "starchitects," as they're called. It's a revolving door of Frank Gehry, Rem Koolhass, Peter Eisenman and a bunch of other people. The results have been disastrous for practically every place that's done this.

Rem Koolhaas: The Architect of Menace

JHK: The case of the Seattle Central Library is interesting. It's designed by Rem Koolhass. He's a Dutch architect who is much esteemed as the great wizard of whatever post-post-post-modern condition we've entered. He was given a chair at the Harvard Graduate School of Design, their architecture school. And for the last ten years, just about every great commission internationally has been dumped on him, including the Seattle library.

It's a pretty monstrous building. On the outside it's this big chunky crystalline UFO that looks like something that Keanu Reeves should step out of to inform the world that civilization as we know it is ending. It's a monstrous, hard-edged, glassy, steely heap that communicates very poorly with the street.

The inside of it is organized so weirdly that the whole idea you get

---

Beautiful Buildings

A businessman would not have dared to put up a hideous building in Troy in 1911. It was part of the software in the hard drive of their brain that required them to do this. We didn't have to twist their arm with design review boards or codes that forced them to do stuff. They did it because it was the right thing to do and because it was part of their culture.

—James Howard Kunstler, June 11, 2009
KunstlerCast #68: "Historic Preservation"

from Rem Koolhaas is that he's striving to confuse the person using the building and create as much anxiety as possible in the users. The object of this whole exercise is to make the architect seem more supernaturally brilliant for having created all these mystifications—the more mystification they create, the more it supposedly means that they know things that you don't.

The starchitects say that this anarchic idea of trying to disturb the citizen over the building, or defy their expectations, is supposed to be a healthy strategy. But I don't find it healthy at all. I think people need to be oriented and comfortable in their surroundings. The buildings need to inform them about where they are, and who they are, and where they're going and what they're doing.

For example, in the Seattle library, he's got some things like staircases that actually get smaller as you go up the stairs, like the psychotic buildings in that German expressionist movie *The Cabinet of Dr. Caligari*. German expressionism was used a lot in the sets of horror movies that emanated from the Weimar Republic—*The Golem* and Fritz Lang's *Metropolis*. It all grows out of the early fascination with psychotherapy and the dark side of human character, and the discovery that the subconscious is a weird and ominous place. So of course they tried to express that in the movie sets they designed. And Koolhass has caught that and done it beautifully. But I don't think people want that done beautifully with their buildings. I don't think people are seeking to be disoriented and confounded by buildings. If anything, they're looking to be well oriented and assured that their culture is a meaningful protective thing. Not some kind of menace. Koolhass specializes in being an architect of menace.

So this is all in the service of grandiosity and narcissism and architects making themselves appear to be something that they aren't: supernatural wizards. We don't need supernatural wizards. We need competent architects who will give us buildings that are neurologically comprehensible, that satisfy our needs for orientation and our even deeper needs for cultural orientation—to know who we are, what culture we're in and what's going on in it.

DC: If you go to a city or town where the buildings were built before the 1940s, you can pretty much identify the post office, the library, the school and the church by the way the building looks. Rem Koolhaas's buildings, and buildings by other starchitects, defy these "typologies," as you say.

JHK: Exactly. That's the word that I've been using a lot. People may not understand what typologies are in buildings, but they're classifications of buildings by their type and what they're intended for and what their programming is. Throughout history, there has been a tendency in architecture for buildings to present themselves typologically in relation to what they do—which enables us to identify them. In the simplest sense, in American culture, we know what a church is supposed to look like, or has looked like over the years. It's a rectangular building with something elevated in the front—we call it a steeple. That's become our signifier for that. Obviously, you don't have to do churches like that. You can do them in other ways. The way we've chosen to do them now, in our time, is we make them look like muffler shops, which isn't so groovy.

DC: What I don't understand is: not only have these guys like Koolhass conned all the mayors of these cities around the world, but the American Institute of Architects is giving this guy awards. Koolhass got an award for the Seattle Central Library.

JHK: All the big architecture prizes are going to these horrendous, despotic, high-tech buildings that look like they're constructed out of Gillette Blue Blades or some other really frightening material.

It's a con game. It's also a game of "The Emperor's New Clothes." These guys are all trying to support an ideology which says, in essence, "The more we can mystify the public, the more brilliant we will appear to be."

Frank Gehry: Tortured Metal Blobs

DC: Another starchitect is Frank Gehry, who also has a building in Seattle, the Experience Music Project, which is an interactive museum for rock 'n' roll.

JHK: The exterior is a wavy, weird, torqued-out, tortured-looking facade. One of the things Frank Gehry got real excited about was computer-aided design, which has allowed architects to torture every surface because the computer does all the math and figures out exactly what the engineering has to be for all these tortured metal claddings and steel structural stuff that has to be fabricated. It goes straight from the computer to the fabrication computer and then they make it.

DC: It looks like what you might get if you made a building out of Salvador Dali's melting clocks.

JHK: Plus it's got all kinds of weird colors. It's literally what the building affects to represent: "experience music." The idea is that's what you see in your mind when music is playing, so there are all these weird shapes and colors. I'm sorry, my mind is not a roller coaster blob of tortured metal.

DC: It's in a fairground type area in Seattle, though, so it's not disastrous to have a building like that in a setting like that. Unfortunately a lot of Gehry's other buildings, which are similarly bizarre, are not sealed off in amusement park areas of the cities. And they look freakish.

JHK: By the way, the starchitects promote incomprehensible buildings. But when it comes down to it, they want to live in traditional buildings themselves. People like Robert Venturi and Denise Scott Brown, who were famous for their polemical tract in the 1970s called *Learning from Las Vegas*, this seminal book about how wonderful Las Vegas was in its early sixties or mid-sixties incarnation with the Frank Sinatra-type hotels which are all gone now. They were reveling in the glories of the parking lot and the way that the car related to the town and all the mid-twentieth-century crapola which they elevated to iconic status and formed another absurd branch of modern or post-modern etiology. They were famous for that kind of stuff and yet they lived in a very traditional neocolonial house in the Philadelphia suburbs. That's true of a lot of architects.

The Role of Monumental Architecture

DC: Instead of trying to mystify the public, what should these star architects be doing with these huge projects?

JHK: There's a different path. One way of understanding the urban principles involved is to know that there's a difference between background buildings and monumental buildings. Monumental buildings have a certain obligation to help us feel oriented, to know what they are, to be typologically consistent with our expectations, and also to present a sense of decorum to the city.

The city can be an intimidating place. It's a place where you're meeting a lot of strangers, constantly. There are a lot of exciting, stimulating, but also intimidating things that happen to you in the city. So one of the purposes of architecture, for a few thousand years, has been to reassure us that when we're in the city, we're in a place that is safe, in which transactions occur that we can understand. We're in surroundings that are coherent. The outsides of the buildings embellish and honor the public realm. Good architecture honors our presence in the public realm by speaking to us in languages and vocabularies and syntaxes and grammars and rhythms and patterns that we understand from our own culture.

So when you bring into that setting this effort to mystify and confuse everybody and deliberately create more anxiety, you're doing a real disservice, not only to the individual people who inhabit the place, but to the idea of civic life as a general proposition.

The Mother Ship

DC: We have a new galactic battleship that just arrived in my city here in Troy. It's the EMPAC building on the Rensselaer Polytechnic Institute campus. EMPAC stands for "Experimental Media and Performing Arts Center," by the way. It was designed by a minor starchitect.[1] Have you seen this building yet?

JHK: Yes, it's the mother ship.

DC: It's a big glass box on the hill with a large wooden sphere inside it, which is a concert hall. To get into this giant spider egg in the center, you cross over a chasm on these catwalk-bridges like you're Obi-Wan Kenobi deactivating the tractor beam. The main stairs of the building get narrower as you go up them and it feels like this huge orb is going to roll over and squash you at any minute.

JHK: The tragic thing about it is that the RPI campus is one of the more coherent ensembles of urban college buildings in the United States. Most of it is a Beaux-Arts period, Greco-Roman, neoclassical ensemble of buildings. It's very handsome, very orderly. It creates a sense of coherence, which helps young people— who are struggling to develop a point of view about the world—to feel that their existence has purpose and order. The experience in these settings is enhanced by being surrounded by buildings that reflect a certain amount of coherence. Into this, they've now introduced this mother ship UFO. But it's perfectly consistent with the trend of what's gone on in every campus in every city in America.

DC: It's not just disrupting the coherence of the college buildings, though, because the campus happens to be perched on top of a hill—so the college buildings are the skyline of my city. And now we have this structure up there that they've been blasting green and red spotlights on at night, like, "Look at this thing."

JHK: Yeah, it's like if you were to put on a clown suit and jump up and down on the highest part of your city and point at yourself and say, "Look at me, I'm special." By the way, we should now have a Special Olympics for architects so they can jump up and down in their clown suits and be as a special as they want.

DC: They have a school of architecture at RPI. What are these architects learning in school?

JHK: You can probably count on one hand the architecture schools around the country that are actually teaching something that has a future. Most of them are stuck in the fashionista/mystification racket. And RPI, unfortunately, is one of them. Although there they have an even heavier emphasis on some of the technical considerations, like these claddings that are made out of rare metals like titanium, which is an unbelievable squandering of resources. They're really into a lot of the high-tech stuff.

Many of the buildings that are getting these awards from the architecture societies and the Pritzker Prize are doing it by dabbling in high-techism. There is not necessarily anything wonderful about cladding a building with titanium, from a technical point of view. It doesn't improve the insulating or heating properties or air-conditioning properties. It's just a stunt really.

DC: Jim, you lecture all around the country and you do speak to —

JHK: I actually call it "flapping my gums."

DC: But you do speak at some architectural institutes and things like that?

JHK: Yeah, I've been to many of the biggies.

DC: So have you talked to these architects? What the hell are they learning in school? Do they feel ashamed of their profession when they hear you speak? Or do they argue with you?

JHK: They argue with me strenuously, especially at the more elite universities. I've been to Harvard three or four times. They think that mystification is wonderful. It makes them feel more superior. They're totally along with that program and they're certainly prompted and supported in it by their professors, who also get a huge lift out of feeling like superior supernatural beings from another planet. They've succeeded in mystifying people and making them feel uncomfortable in the buildings that they have to go to everyday. And they think that this is a joke that I'm complaining about it.

DC: College campuses seem to be fertile ground for your monthly critiques of architectural eyesores.

JHK: I frequently feature college buildings, especially new ones, on the "Eyesore of the Month" department of my website, because they seem to represent what's worst in current architectural practice and in our culture as a whole.

Brutalism

Duncan Crary: There's another style of modern architecture out there that's pretty awful called "brutalism." These are the buildings made entirely from poured concrete. I have a brutalist building down the block from where I live, Troy City Hall, which is in the process of being taken down.

James Howard Kunstler: Yay! There might be a celebration when you're finally rid of this despotic presence in your town.

DC: It's already started. Tell me how

this particular style of architecture came about in the first place.

JHK: It's funny that it even got that name, "brutalism." It derives from a French term describing the use of raw concrete as the main motif for the building's design—the brutal raw concrete. It's also in the spirit of form meets function and supposedly giving an honest treatment of the materials that you're using—not trying to disguise them behind any decoration or ornament.

So these are typically those raw concrete buildings all over America that date from about 1965 to 1980.

Hysterical Historical Preservation

Why has the historic preservation movement been as hysterical to save things as they have in the last thirty years? The answer, I think, is pretty clear: we're not capable of putting new things up that are as good as the old things we're losing. It's hard to account for that. We're not dumber than our great grandparents, and we're certainly a lot richer than they were, or at least we have been for the last three or four or five decades. So it's not as if we lacked resources.

But there were forces in our economy and culture that have prevented us from putting up buildings that are as worthy of our affection as these things that we're losing. So consequently, there's this hysteria to save every scrap of anything, really, before the Second World War.

—James Howard Kunstler, June 11, 2009
KunstlerCast #68: "Historic Preservation"

My college campus was full of them, and they were ghastly. I have a vivid memory from back in 1969 of being in a stairwell in the new communications building at my college, which was a classic brutalismo, and feeling like I was in the elevator to hell—that this thing was designed absolutely on purpose to make you feel bad as you were going up or down the stairs, to be as grim and dreary as possible, like going into a dungeon.[2] There was certainly a lot of cachet at the time about this whole idea of expressing the strength and rawness of the concrete and the honesty of it all. But it ended up producing buildings that were broadly disliked.

DC: How would you describe a typical brutalist building—what it looks like, the texture and the size and the shape and the structure?

JHK: They're very emphatically boxes, concrete boxes. It's funny because Troy City Hall looks like a mini Boston City Hall. They're both just square boxes with a lot of raw concrete defining the doors and windows. Boston City Hall kind of floats. It was designed to look as though it was levitating on its site. Once you get above that, you get these massive concrete members.

DC: And the texture, the surface of the concrete is unfinished. You can see little holes and imperfections.

JHK: Yeah. What you get on the surface is from the forms that were used to mold the concrete as it was poured in.

DC: It looks unfinished.

JHK: That's the whole point. It's supposed to be honest. Of course that's the strange thing, because you would think from its appearance that this stuff is massively strong, but in fact the iron rebar at the center is melting away month by month and year by year.

DC: Yeah, Troy City Hall has this massive parking accessory unit that goes along with it. But the city had to close it a while ago because large chunks of concrete were falling from the ceiling onto the parked cars. You could see the exposed and rusting rebar.

JHK: Exactly. This kind of raw concrete construction tends to disintegrate surprisingly fast. It looks so strong that it's like the *Führerbunker*, or some kind of massive thing meant to withstand cluster bombs. Then you turn around and thirty or forty years later, the building's shot. So we end up being surprised that these big massive things have such poor integrity.

DC: Was it known at the time of construction that these brutalist buildings were not going to last long?

JHK: I think that, to some degree, they just didn't care because we had really entered the heart of the period when we just disposed of stuff. We didn't care about how long stuff lasted, whether it was automobiles or houses or institutional buildings, because we were going to throw them away anyway and build something else within a couple of generations.

DC: You believe it's unacceptable for buildings to only last one generation.

JHK: It's pathetic. So much about contemporary architecture has been experimental that the people who design and build these things don't really know what the outcome is going to be. This is one of the problems when you're not emulating prior success. It becomes even more problematical now as we face really serious resource constraints that are not going away.

So we do all this innovation, but we don't necessarily know what the outcome is going to be with some new material. It's only been in the last hundred years that we recovered enough skill with concrete to even get to the same place where the Romans were at.

Ruinenwert, Nazis and Neoclassicism

DC: What happens to all that concrete once they knock down these buildings, or these buildings fall down on their own? Can you reuse it for anything, or does it just get thrown into a landfill?

JHK: You can't grind it up and make new concrete. I don't know what we're going to do with it. It may resist any of our wishes because it will be too expensive to demolish.

A lot of this stuff may be the ruins of the future.

DC: Maybe we can line the train track beds with it when we start to rebuild our rail system.

JHK: That's one possibility. There's an interesting story, by the way, about Adolf Hitler's building adventures in Berlin—or at least his ambitions, which were mostly not realized. He was going to rebuild Berlin into a great German Reich capital that he called Germania. It included these enormous halls for his public appearances, one of them a giant dome three times the size of the Astrodome in Houston.

Hitler was going to do all this, and he was very close to his pet architect, Albert Speer, who later went on to be an important functionary in the last years of the Nazi party. He was Hitler's kind of soul mate in architectural ambition. They arrived at a theory, which they called *ruinenwert*, which is one of those German compound words. It means "ruin value"—the value of ruins. They were thinking about what the residue of the Third Reich would be in a thousand years when, like the Roman Empire, it came to an end. They wanted to leave some really wonderful ruins behind. And they knew that reinforced concrete was not going to work very well—that it was going to leave unattractive ruins. So they decided that they weren't going to build in reinforced concrete, and instead just do everything in limestone and granite.

DC: That's a pretty fascinating long-term outlook.

JHK: The fact that they got down to such a level of insane detail about worrying about the quality of the ruins that they left behind—it's so fantastically weird. When you ramp up an imperial venture like that, I guess those kinds of considerations come in.

DC: Were the buildings that the Nazis created ornamented in a more classical style, like Roman architecture?

JHK: Sort of. The Beaux-Arts had passed by when Hitler came along, and what was left in the 1930s was stripped down neoclassicism, which was kind of like art deco, where you still get gestures and forms toward classicism, but they're simplified. That's the last iteration, the last gasp of classicism within Western civilization, whether it represents the demonic Nazi party or anybody.

When the war is over, even the remnant of classicism is identified with tyranny and Nazism and despotism, and we reject that. By the time we're getting into the 1950s in the United States, neoclassicism is so discredited because it's been thoroughly identified not just with Nazism but also with the Communists. So nobody wants to get near it. Modernism in all of its various styles and iterations becomes the architectural expression of decency and democracy.

DC: It's ironic that modernism ended up producing so many despotic forms of architecture—concrete bunkers, glass fishbowls, menacing blobs.

JHK: It's incredibly ironic, and I had that feeling when I went to Berlin. On the west side of Berlin, which was the free democratic side, they had to rebuild all the cultural infrastructure that had been on the Communist side of the city—the great art museum, the great symphony hall, the opera house were all behind the wall. And they rebuilt it not only according to modernism, but along this street network that was all curvilinear and made no sense within the street network of Berlin. In fact the concert hall was such a bizarre building that it has been nicknamed the pregnant oyster ever since.[3]

The Effort to Save Brutalism from the Wrecking Ball

DC: It's hard to believe but there are historic preservationists out there trying to save brutalist buildings from being demolished. There was a story on NPR about a group who effectively blocked the demolition of a brutalist church in Washington, D.C., called the "Third Church."[4] It's a ridiculous building from the 1970s with one window, no steeple. The church bells are hanging from a slab of concrete sticking out from the side. The poor congregation wants to replace the building with something that better serves their needs and actually represents their practices and beliefs. But they claimed in this news story that they can't demolish the building—or even change it—because a group of preservationists had the building designated a historic landmark…unbeknownst to the congregation itself.

That's the other part of the story I find kind of hard to believe, personally. Because there are plenty of buildings on the National Register of Historic Places that get knocked down all the time. But the preservationists have somehow prevented that from happening in this case.

JHK: Yeah, this has become a trend in certain parts of the country.

DC: To save this stuff?

JHK: Yeah, because the fact of the matter is, it *is* historic now—"historical."

DC: Ugh.

JHK: I know it's sad to imagine, but that's where we're at. I remind you that this is something that's going on in a particularly strange time in history. Where it's coming from probably is that the historic preservationists have ties to academia. Historic preservation is now a profession, and it's often taught as a subgroup in the architecture schools. And the academic architecture professors all have an intellectual investment in supporting the stuff that was done in the last fifty years, in supporting the legitimacy of it. So you get a mutually reinforcing system where the academics are tied in with the historic preservationists. The situation might be quite different in thirty years or fifty years when the brutalist buildings themselves are so beyond repair and really represent something that comes to be despised by future generations.

DC: I should add that the story about the church—it's not just an aesthetics issue.

JHK: It's an ideological issue.

DC: Yeah. It is an ugly building. But the aesthetics are creating a functional problem for the church. Churches are supposed to be welcoming. But this building doesn't welcome. You can't even tell what it is from the outside, so people don't even know it's a church. No one who doesn't already belong to the congregation is coming inside to pray or worship or to see what this congregation is all about. Even if you are worshipping inside, it's like worshipping in a parking garage. And apparently the concrete the building is made of is so porous that it reeks of mildew inside.

So the arguments against this particular brutalist building, and against brutalism in general, are not just about aesthetics. That's the way some people try to dismiss arguments against this type of stuff, right? They say aesthetics are subjective and therefore they discredit legitimate complaints.

Arguing Aesthetics

JHK: So many of the common arguments you hear on a small-town design review board end up being just personal taste biases or fashion biases, and it's unfortunate. It ends up being a solipsistic issue.

DC: I do want to address the issue of beauty itself, though, beautiful buildings. I know it's slightly subjective, but it's also an important matter that I don't think should be dismissed. These buildings are almost universally recognized as being ugly. And you have said before that we must build beautiful buildings to honor our existence—that's the purpose of beautiful buildings. Why is it important to honor our existence?

JHK: We have to feel that our mission in existence—not just as animals on some third-rate planet, but this whole project of civilization—has some dignity and some meaning. So we want to confer a sense of dignity and purpose on it. I think that's understandable. We want to make it something that's worthy of our affection. Even if it's just among us, let alone what the cosmic forces, like the hypothetical figures like God, might think of what we're doing.

I think we want it to reflect the best of all we've discovered about our own cognitive processes and the human brain, and our values, and everything that goes into making us worth being here and worth continuing. I don't think it's a good thing at all for a group of beings to have a self-esteem problem, to think that they're not worth being on the planet they inhabit.

There's perhaps an additional question as to why raw concrete may or may not be beautiful. To some people no doubt it is. There are certain kinds of Japanese ceramics that are designed to be very raw on purpose and are considered to be very beautiful in their own way. There probably are elements of even some of these brutalist buildings that we detest that have some kind of appeal to them. They are not totally devoid of appeal. But on the whole I think there are things about them that we recognize as being not friendly for us, and not friendly for our future and for our spirits. They drag us down and degrade us, and they have a baleful kind of personality.

Aside from the sheer cynicism of the fashion-directed impulses of the architecture scene in the late twentieth century, it is a little bit hard to understand why people would get off with fashioning things that are inherently baleful. I suppose it's part of the whole ethos of being cool.

DC: Brutalism does not honor our existence.

JHK: I don't think so—we can tell from the eagerness that people show to tear it down. Even though there may be some historic preservation strictures against doing that, I don't think very many tears are going to be shed when these things go.

Turquoise, Panelized Crap from the 1960s

I go to towns all over the United States and there's still this residue of these turquoise panels over everything. Every town in America bought a ton of this stuff and they slapped it on all their old buildings, rather than maintain the older ornaments. We're still peeling that stuff off all over the United States.

To some degree, we'll probably be returning to regional materials found in nature. The more important buildings will be made of masonry, stone, brick—the traditional materials. Once you get into that you start getting back into levels of skill which can produce something more interesting than a turquoise aluminum panel-clad four-story motor vehicle bureau.

—James Howard Kunstler, June 11, 2009
KunstlerCast #68: "Historic Preservation"

Chapter 5: Getting There

Making Other Arrangements

Duncan Crary: I have a car, which I don't really drive very often. I keep it parked on a city street several blocks outside of downtown where I live. It's a convenience sometimes, but most of the time it's a nuisance. I have to keep checking on it and moving it from one side of the street to the other. I have to pay to maintain it and to have insurance. I've been thinking about other options for car ownership. We don't have any around me, but I've been looking into things like Zipcar and car clubs.

James Howard Kunstler: The Zipcar is an American manifestation of the "car clubs" which are popular in Europe. The idea of the car club is you don't have to go through all the grief of car ownership and maintenance and payment. You join this club for like $800 a year and anytime you need a car to go on an excursion, or go on a picnic in the country, or go to a store and bring something bulky home, or move to a new apartment, you go out and you get one of these vehicles from the car club. They have many kinds of different vehicles—sporty vehicles for excursions, pickup trucks if you need to move your stuff and so on.

It would seem to be a sensible thing here in the US. But, remember, you have to have the whole social urbanistic and architectural infra-structure in place for that to work. It works fine in Amsterdam, Holland, because Amsterdam is a wonderful, walkable city. They never destroyed their traditional urban pattern. People are living in row houses and apartments fairly close together and well integrated with all the shopping, entertainment, civic, cultural and educational stuff, all mixed in very richly. They're not prevented from making an excursion by living like that. Any time you want a car, you go down and get a car from the car club and you drive out to the countryside.

You know, in America we all have our own cars at our disposal all the time, but because of that, there's almost no place in America that's worth being in or going to. That's one

---

Segway

The Segway was a good idea for people who are disabled, let's say, for one reason or another; too old. But the idea that normal people need a prosthetic extension for walking around, that was also kind of nuts. It's just another personal transportation device that costs a huge amount of money, like $3,000 or something. Was it better than a bicycle?

—James Howard Kunstler May 8, 2008
KunstlerCast #13: "Green Buildings"

of the unintended consequences of mass automobile use, you actually destroy the terrain so voraciously that nowhere is worth driving to. The other one, of course, is it's estimated to cost somewhere around $8,000 a year to keep any car on the road, between the payments, the maintenance, the insurance and the fuel. That's generally the going rate.[1] So if you're only paying a thousand bucks a year to belong to a car club and you can have one anytime you need one—and you don't have to worry about storing it, parking it or insuring—great!

DC: If they could only get a critical mass for the need in my town, I would join a car club.

JHK: In the United States, it's going to be a problem because by the time we have a critical mass for that stuff, the whole motoring scene may be in complete disarray. Between the oil problems and the problems of people affording cars in any form, the failure of the car-dependency system is going to be epic. We're going to be able to mitigate it somewhat with schemes to work around it, like the jitney busses in the third world where people take their personal transportation and turn it into some kind of a shuttle. But the final reckoning with car-dependency and the suburbia that goes with it is going to be one of those epic changes in human affairs, at least for America.

DC: I met some people at the Congress for the New Urbanism this summer who worked for car-sharing companies here in the US. One was a small local company in Madison, Wisconsin, and the other was a national outfit based in Chicago. Apparently car sharing is on the rise in the US. So is ride sharing, which is like a formal hitchhiking/carpooling

Road Trip!

For me, most of the enjoyment of the road trip actually comes in the anticipation of it. In a way, it's an anticipation of being liberated from the routines of your humdrum everyday life. What we're talking about is just the same age-old American Dream of the liberty of the road— the freedom of the open road. It even goes back to the pre-automobile age, with Walt Whitman singing the "Song of the Open Road." This is a very strong theme in American life.

Now for us, the practical reality of it is, yeah we're on the open road, but it's the New York State Thruway. It's flat. It's boring. There are almost no human artifacts to see except the broken-down residue of a farm or something. We don't even have the experience of stopping to get something to eat or drink in a place that has any character, because they're all just thruway rest stops and they're all the same. So even that element of it is monotonous and boring.

But I guess part of the romance of the open road is the idea that you're going to have a sequence of new adventures and that you'll encounter strange, interesting and wonderful new things. We're not likely to do that on the New York State Thruway—I mean unless we see an incredibly gruesome accident, or get in one ourselves.

—James Howard Kunstler, January 12, 2010
KunstlerCast #96: "Road Trip!"
En route to Rochester, New York

program where you don't necessarily know the people you're riding with. One place where they do this is Washington, D.C., with the "slugging."[2]

JHK: These are workarounds and we'll see that for a while. Right now we're just discovering how you work around stuff. I do think that the bright side of workarounds is that they exercise your ability to be creative and resilient. And that's one of the things we're going to see more of: very interesting local resiliency.

Reinvesting in Rail

Duncan Crary: One of the projects that you advocate for is restoring passenger rail in the US.

James Howard Kunstler: As I am fond of saying about the American railroad situation, we have a train system that the Bulgarians would be ashamed of. But the railroad situation is serious in a number of ways. There is probably no project that would have a greater effect on reducing our oil use right away than fixing the passenger railroad system in America. It would have the greatest effect on our gas consumption of anything we could do. It would put scores of thousands of people to work at meaningful jobs at all levels. It would benefit people in all ranks of society. It does not require any new technology, and the fact that we haven't been talking about it shows what a nation of clowns we really are, how unserious we are about our problems. I can't overstate how important this is, because the airlines are dying—they are visibly disintegrating around us. You're not going to be able to visit granny in Louisville if we don't get the train system running again.

DC: At least President Obama has started to pay attention to passenger rail. Too bad the money he's putting toward it is only a tiny fraction of what he's putting into fixing the highway system.

JHK: I wish that we could have made it a condition of bailing out the auto companies that they would start some kind of manufacturing of the rolling stock that we need to run on the rails. Because obviously, they're not tooled up for it now. But it wouldn't take that much. They do have the large assembly buildings, and lines, and the robots and the equipment.

DC: When the Obama Administration first announced their plans to reinvest in our national rail system there was some confusion about their use of the term "high-speed."

JHK: I was deceived myself when

Mass Transit

I prefer to use the term public transit rather than mass transit. Because just in casual conversation with people, or in formal conversation in city council chambers, whenever you invoke the word "mass transit," it seems to summon up the idea of communism and Joseph Stalin and pushing people around. That's not what public transit is all about. It's not about forcing you to do stuff.

—James Howard Kunstler, September 16, 2010
KunstlerCast #125: "Cassandra"

the Obama proposal for rail was released. They billed it as "high-speed" rail. What I said at the time was that it's crazy to build a separate high-speed rail network that would be an additional layer of tracks over what we've got already—because true high-speed rail can't run on the kind of tracks we now have. I think we need to demonstrate that we can do this on the Bulgarian level first before we get that techno-grandiose.

But what they were talking about was fixing up the existing rail networks and then running trains over 100 mph. That's not really high-speed to people in the world today. So in a way, they're being a little grandiose. But if what they're really looking to do is to rebuild the railroad network we have, then we have to applaud that effort because it's exactly what we need to do.

We had a regular railroad system in the US that was the envy of the world. We had a lot of trains running over 100 mph in 1925 on tracks that were then not very old. In fact, many of them were pretty darn new. If we can get back to that level of service, we would benefit hugely.

DC: The speed issue seems to dominate the discussion. But it's probably more important to keep the trains on time at whatever speed they're running at.

JHK: One of the reasons that nobody wants to take a train from New York City to Chicago instead of flying is because it's uniformly seven hours late. People just won't tolerate that.

Light Rail

DC: We're still pouring money into fixing the highways right now with the stimulus package. It seems like there's plenty of room within those highway corridors to include light rail.

JHK: Sure. We do have the median strips, and, indeed, we do have the extra lanes.

DC: Would you support the effort to rebuild the nation's highways if we cut down on some of the lanes and converted those lanes into light rail for short-distance, intercity travel?

JHK: I'm not even convinced that you'd have to cut down on the lanes. Probably the best thing we could do right away would be to start a couple of experimental lines in places like our region, running from Albany to Schenectady, Troy and through the corridor heading into the North Country.

DC: These are all small cities relatively close to each other of not even 100,000 people living in the core. So the ridership may not be that large.

JHK: No, but these places were magnificently connected by light rail once. The US had an interurban transit system apart from the heavy rail passenger system that was also the envy of the world at the turn of the previous century. In the real heyday of the streetcar era, which was about 1890 to about 1925 or so, we had a fantastic parallel system of light rails that went all over the place. The interurban trolley lines would get you from Boston to Wisconsin with only one twenty-mile interruption, which was located in New York State, oddly enough. Back in the 1920s, that's how comprehensive the system was. And we were a poorer society then than we are now, even with our financial meltdown and banking calamity. So the idea that we can't build something like this is really preposterous.

The bottom line is, we do have these corridors that are now being devoted to cars. It seems to me that we could try at least a few experimental light rail lines. Whether it's in our region, or going from Atlanta to Chattanooga, or from Dayton to Columbus, Ohio, there are plenty of opportunities to do this all over the country. And it would be heartwarming to see us do something other than just fix bridges and tunnels.

Dallas, Texas, built a light rail line about nine years ago and they had very low expectations for it. But the ridership has really been quite high. Portland, Oregon, is another place that made some really large investments in light rail and I think those have proved to work out really well. Everywhere that we've seen it, light rail is paying off.

Rails to Trails

DC: What's your take on these rails-to-trails initiatives, when they take an old, abandoned railbed and turn it into a bike trail?

JHK: As bike trails, they are rather rewarding places. But you can't do it without having a nagging feeling that the whole thing was a fiasco— that, yeah, it is nice to ride on a dedicated bike trail, but we have taken the railroad system in America and thrown it away. On the other hand, you could think of these rails-to-trails projects as a form of land banking. Because you could refurbish the rights-of-way—they're still there. In fact, it's a good thing that they still exist as corridors. It is not that difficult to rebuild a track bed and a railbed and to put the tracks on top of it. I imagine in the future we will.

By the way, there's no reason why you can't have a bike trail running parallel to a rail trail. Of course it means you will be disturbed by a train going by periodically, but it won't be like being on an interstate highway.

Water Transit

Duncan Crary: Jim, you're anticipating a big revival of water transit in the years ahead. What do you see the role of water transportation being in the US in the next fifty, sixty years?

James Howard Kunstler: A lot of projections of the future are predicated on the idea that all the conditions of the present are going to continue. That we're going to continue to have air freight and that the commercial aviation industry is going to function the same way. That we're going to continue to have container shipping. That globalism as we know it will remain the same. And that we'll continue to have the trucking system. I don't think that any of these things are true.

My version of the future is that it's going to be about transporting things by boat and on water. The inland waterways are going to be the place where the action is, because for a while I think that the American economy is going to be much more inwardly focused on continental activity. It doesn't mean that we won't have trade with other countries, but I don't think that globalism is going to continue in nearly the exuberant way that we've known it.

Cities in the future are going to be organized around their waterways in ways that they're not now. One thing that means is that we're not going to build a lot of glittering condo towers on the waterfront. We've got to put the infrastructure back on the riverfronts for ships and boats—everything from the dry docks where they fix the boats, to the warehouses where they store the goods, to the counting houses where you have the back offices for the shippers. All that stuff is going to have to go back.

I don't know what's going to happen to our canal system. We have this fabulous inland waterway system in America. Much of it is still there and a lot of it is in pretty good shape. The New York State Canal System has been kept in immaculate condition. I went to a canal outside of Chicago, in a place called Lockport, Illinois, and I was impressed with that.[3] It connects Chicago at Lake Michigan to the Mississippi-Ohio-Missouri river system. It's still in excellent condition.

I think in the future, when we're strapped for oil and mechanical energy and it becomes harder to run big earth-moving machines, then the canals may become very important again. A lot of it depends on whether we're going to be able to rebuild the rail system, because the canals to some extent were put out of business in the 1850s by the growth and development of the railroad.

There's still a lot of freight moving on rail in this country. We have a few lines in America now that are carrying a lot of freight, and in particular a lot of coal to electric power plants. But what we had before 1950 was a much richer network of rails that went to every little town in America. Those are the lines that don't exist any more and those are the ones we would have to put back.

I don't know if there will be some combination of railroads, canals, rivers and navigable waterways. One thing I am confident about, though, is that we're not going to have the kind of trucking industry that we've enjoyed for the last eighty years. And we're probably not going to have the same kind of private car ownership system that we've gotten used to. But emergently we are going to have to find new ways to move stuff and people around.

DC: What do you see happening to all the old communities that were built along our inland waterways? Right now a lot of them aren't doing so well.

JHK: We do have great inland waterway cities like St. Louis, Cincinnati and Kansas City that have really withered in many ways. Those are the places I think are going to come back. They're not going to come back as skyscraper condo cities though. The waterfronts of these places may actually be pretty disorderly.

People who work on waterfronts, longshoreman and sailors—they're not necessarily the most appealing people in the working world, and they bring certain things with them:

vices, prostitution, gambling, cheap housing. So we got this idea over the years in American cities that waterfronts are disagreeable places. That's one of the reasons we sanitized them and made such an effort to remove all the infrastructure that was there and replace it with sparkling parks and bikeways and rock 'n' roll bandshells and condominiums. We basically went in there and disinfected the waterfronts.

We're going to have to rebuild the facilities for the infrastructure for doing this activity again. That means we're going to have to make room again for the warehouses and the piers and the sleazy accommodations for the sailors. We're not even thinking about it now. It's so far off the radar screen. But the current situation in America is just laughable. Manhattan Island, which is probably the most amazing protected deep-water harbor in the United States if not the world—I don't think it has a single activated pier or facility on the whole island anymore.

DC: They have restaurants on the few remaining piers now and things like that.

JHK: Yeah, or tennis clubs. The island of Manhattan used to bristle with docks all the way from the Upper West Side clear around to the Battery to the East Side. It was bristling with piers and activity. That's all gone. But it's only moved about five miles west to Elizabeth, New Jersey, because of the nature of container shipping and the fact that you need a certain kind of infrastructure for the cranes that have to unload these giant steel boxes and then stack them up in these vast parking lots for the steel boxes. So you need a lot of space of a type that wasn't available on the West Side piers of Manhattan. It doesn't mean that New York isn't a seaport anymore, it just means that we suburbanized the shipping activity. But I think that's gonna change.

Chapter 6: The City in Mind

The Green Metropolis?

Duncan Crary: There's a lot of talk about "green" buildings these days, and the idea that living in skyscrapers is supposedly a "green" way of life. You're not too keen on skyscrapers to begin with but you're also not thrilled with the "green" building movement right now, are you?

James Howard Kunstler: I'm not comfortable with the term "green" as applied to these issues, because it's become a meaningless buzzword that's supposed to stand for a sense of having a future. It's consistent with our tendency to just use public relations to make everything all right. Unfortunately, "green" also has the subconscious effect of making people think that if you only ruralize the city, it'll be better because it'll be "greener"—there will be more plants there. I don't know if that's the correct way to think about this at all. I would prefer to frame the whole issue in terms of whether our cities and our living places have a future or not.

DC: There's also a lot of greenwashing out there, labeling things to be environmentally friendly when they're not really.

JHK: I have a very dear friend—a hippie carpenter who morphed into a developer—and he did a so-called green development, full of buildings that were impeccably built without any kind of artificial off-gassing insulation. It was pristine. The trouble is that it's built in a cul-de-sac subdivision, which is going to require mandatory driving and is not connected to any other kind of civic activity or infrastructure.

So I'm not impressed with the so-called green thinking that I see. A lot of it is being applied to skyscrapers—which I happen to think is a building type that will be associated with the fossil fuel age and probably should not be built anymore for reasons that go beyond that. I think they generally overburden and distort the urban fabric by putting too many people on one footprint.

DC: You went to New York to take part in a panel discussion about this idea that Manhattan, with all its skyscrapers, is "the greenest place in America." What happened there?

Green Yammer

There's so much yammer about greening this and being green. Everybody wants to be green. I think we're blowing a lot of green smoke up our ass.

—James Howard Kunstler, May 8, 2008
KunstlerCast #13: "Green Buildings"

"Green Skyscrapers"

JHK: The National Arts Club organized a panel discussion with David Owen about his new book *Green Metropolis*, which is somewhat controversial, I suppose, among the architectural community down there. Although for us peak oilsters and collapseniks it's not terribly big news.

David Owen is a *New Yorker* staff writer. About six years ago, he published an article that was very influential.[1] What he said was that Manhattan was the greenest living arrangement in America. And that if you could just stack people up in apartment buildings, then that would be the greatest way for people to live and it would solve all our problems. I'm really simplifying this.

Then he turned the magazine article into a full-fledged book, *Green Metropolis*. I think he's had some time to refine and rethink his basic idea. He seems to have backed away somewhat from the stacking people up in apartments as being this sole animating purpose for his position, and he's taken, more or less, the New Urbanist position that you have to create walkable neighborhoods that are dense. I think we both agree that what's missing from most of the dialogue is the notion that the walkable neighborhood has to be a very big part of the answer to this calamity we face.

There are a couple of points of argument that I have with David Owen and with a couple of the other guys who were there. There were two other architects at the panel from Robert A.M. Stern's office in New York, which does big projects all over the world in places like New York and Melbourne, Australia.[2] They're off on a green building jag now, but unfortunately their green buildings are green megastructures—green skyscrapers and green landscrapers. I have a real beef with that.

Part of the issue is: are we going to have a serious debate about skyscrapers, and towers, and megastructures? Because we really have to stop going that way—we have to stop designing, planning and building megastructures. We have to start thinking about rebuilding our cities at a much finer grain, probably at a lower height— they can still be very dense, though. Nobody goes to Barcelona or central Paris and complains about a lack of cosmopolitan verve in these places.

DC: What is your position against skyscrapers?

JHK: Those of us who have been talking about these things for a while, when we talked about the scale of the city and how it was going to turn out

in decades ahead, we were preoccupied with the energy issues. There was a lot of concern about what the electrical and natural gas equation is going to be for big cities, because it's imperative to have natural gas if you're going to run fifty-story apartment buildings. It's another one of those things that calls into question whether we can run all these megastructures the way that we're expecting to. But something else has entered the picture now—the question of whether these tower buildings will ever be renovated, or whether they are renovate-able.

The Great Tragedy of the Skyscraper City

JHK: A monumental amount of money was rolled into the infrastructure of Manhattan during this explosion of Wall Street activity over the last twenty years, and a lot of it was applied to fixing real estate and fixing the public realm of New York City. But I think New York has gone through its last major renovation at that scale and it's not going to happen again.

Now we have this new generation of buildings that went up in the last boom and they're very high-tech. A lot of them are glass buildings, with glass curtain walls, and they're made of pretty exotic fabricated modular materials. I don't think we're going to have the money to repair them. The financial crisis that we're going through now is not over and what it will represent in the long run will be a very long and comprehensive loss of capital to do the things that we would like to do.

So it's really weird to see the architects, like the two architects at the National Arts Club, give a presentation about building a brand new sky-scraper that looks kinda weird—this big glass flying wing that they've proposed for Battery Park City, for some empty parcel there. It's this elegant, sweeping-glass, wing-like structure—they're proposing to build it now and I'm thinking, "You know, that building will never be fixed after its design life wears off. It will be a one-generation building."

That will prove to be the great tragedy of the skyscraper city—that they ended up being throwaway buildings that could not be subject to adaptive reuse. It's true in terms of the materials they're made out of and their size and scale. So how do we get from that way of building to a mentality where we can properly perceive the fabric of the city as a living organism that can renew itself periodically? I don't know how we're going to get there because this stuff has hubris written all over it.

The Fate of Condos

JHK: There's another big question about the experiment of condoization. And I emphasize "experiment" because we've gotta remember this has really never been done before in history, where you have these massive eighty-story skyscrapers—like the one that Frank Gehry just designed for downtown New York—broken up into separate property ownerships and then all organized in a homeowner association governance. You need to do that with a megastructure in order to operate and maintain it. But we've never been in a situation where that kind of organized ownership has gotten into trouble. We've only seen it on the upswing where we were able to get it going. What happens when your economy starts wobbling and twenty thousand hedgefunders lose their jobs? What happens when those buildings start to lose owners and you have a tower with forty-three units in foreclosure, not paying their homeowners' association fee?

This is an experiment that we haven't seen the end of and I think it will end in a lot of tears. The bottom line will be a lot of buildings that no one knows how to take care of because the revenue flows for the governance will not be there and things will not get fixed.

I read somewhere that when empires are about to dissolve, they often build their biggest and most outlandish monuments. And I'm looking at the skyline of New York and all these new starchitect buildings that are going up, thinking, "Yeah, that's exactly what's going on. We're building these great monuments in the twilight of being a wealthy and powerful empire."

The Effects of Gigantism on Human Neurology

So much of what we have constructed in our lifetimes doesn't even exist at a scale that's congenial to human neurology. Gigantism is everywhere. Even in the most common commercial buildings that we go into, the Walmarts and the Target stores, these things exist at fantastic scales. I find them overwhelming. I almost never go into a Walmart if I can possibly help it. The last time I was in there I was astounded and overwhelmed by the size and scale. I found it immediately depressing and discouraging. It all kind of looked like that warehouse at the end of the first Indiana Jones movie, where they show the place that the Ark of the Covenant has been stored by the government, in some warehouse that's like a seven-mile-long corridor with stacks that are seventy feet high. That's a very common experience for people who go into a Home Depot or a Walmart, and you're dwarfed by everything in there. But there's also the common experience of having to traverse a parking lot. It's such a demoralizing thing that you feel like you're in some kind of a death march every time you do it.

—James Howard Kunstler, May 6, 2010
KunstlerCast #110: "Human Scale"

Is NYC Greener than Small Cities?

DC: Do you think New York City is "greener" than, say, where I live here in a little city—Troy, New York? I get into this discussion from time to time, and people are constantly telling me that everything is so much more efficient in Manhattan—that there are more people using less space in New York, that New York has more public transportation options, that the goods from overseas don't have to travel as far from where they're unloaded to where they're consumed.

JHK: There's no question that it's true statistically that New Yorkers, or Manhattanites, use less electricity per person than people in other parts of the country. But of course, econometrics are not the only way of understanding things, and that leads to a peculiar little area that I've no-

ticed lately, which is that in America, we seem to have this idea that just because we can measure things, we can control them, too. Generally, I'm not quite sure that we can.

DC: What makes Manhattan efficient today is not necessarily going to be true in the future?

JHK: Exactly. The equation is going to change pretty drastically, I think. As that occurs, then all these econometric arguments that we're bringing to it are going to be irrelevant.

DC: But as far as how things operate today, you feel that New York is more efficient than a small city like mine, a hundred and fifty miles upriver?

JHK: Sure. But what troubles me is that all of our assumptions are based on the idea that exactly what's happening now is going to continue indefinitely. All of the arrangements, down to things like the trucks delivering the pork chops to the supermarkets—that must be terrifically expensive. Resupplying this island of enormous needs every day, every hour of the day—it's just a huge enterprise, and I'm not sure it's going to be able to continue at that scale.

DC: OK. This is a silly hypothetical, but I want to get down to your philosophy here. Suppose the Martians landed tomorrow with this limitless, magic fuel that burns cleanly, etc., and there are no more peak oil concerns, there are no more global warming concerns, no more financial woes. Then what would you say about building places like Manhattan for their efficiency? Would you support that, or would you still be opposed to the scale and the way it functions?

JHK: I myself am much more comfortable in a lower city. I think the typical European cities are a scale that, for me, is more comfortable.

I'd rather be in a city full of seven-story buildings than in the middle of Manhattan. Although there's no question that Manhattan is very exciting and full of vitality.

I think guys like Nikos Salingaros and maybe Christopher Alexander—and to some extent Leon Krier—have demonstrated that piling and stacking up so many people on one tiny building footprint does have a tendency to badly distort the civic fabric in ways that are not that obvious to us but that end up producing a pernicious outcome. My own intuition is that we would probably be better off—and we would have better cities—if we eschewed the skyscraper.

When all is said and done I feel that skyscrapers will prove to be anomalous building types that came along during a very special point in human history when we did have this cheap energy fiesta. Since it's

Skyscraper Terrarium Farming

We have to cut through the fantasies people are indulging in now, like the idea that we're going to have these vertical skyscraper gardens that are like terrariums. I find that to be just a completely idiotic notion, because the cost of constructing a ten-story terrarium for growing arugula and basil is just totally out of the realm of reality. We can't afford to build these things now. The planet is going broke as far as money is concerned and we're going to have to be very careful about figuring out what is really possible.

Just as there are traditional urban methods and models for building places where we live, there are also traditional methods of doing gardening locally. They all require a certain amount of skill and knowledge, some of which has been lost, but it also depends on re-allocating things and changing laws in some cases—like if people are going to keep chickens in urban neighborhoods. That's something you can do, and it was probably pretty normal before the First World War. But now of course it's been outlawed all over America. So we have to go get under the hood of the regulations and the laws again, and these are some of the things we have to change.

—James Howard Kunstler, June 3, 2010
KunstlerCast #114: "Agrarian Urbanism"

been going on now for four or five generations, it's normal to us. But I don't think we get a sense of how abnormal it really is in the course of history, and that the equations of the future simply aren't going to support that kind of behavior. We're going to have to get back to a scale of things that is different and more consistent with living in a non-fossil-fuel-fiesta type world.

Manhattan is Not a Well-Designed City

JHK: There's something else about Manhattan in particular that probably needs to be said. That for all of its great vitality and the tremendous amount of action, energy and happening stuff that goes on there, it's not a very well-designed city per se—even just in terms of the street and block plan. Once you get above the old Dutch part of the city, beyond Wall Street, it's this monotonous, mechanistic, relentless grid that marches north till it ends up at the Harlem River. And it contains almost none of the devices of urban design that allow people to create places of beauty in other cities. We have very few terminating vistas, very few meaningful small plazas or squares, or places where streets meet in a meaningful way—and even where they do, they don't really define space well.

Times Square is a freakish public place. It's just an odd intersection of a couple of very large boulevards. Herald Square ten blocks south is the same thing. They're not really deliberately created public places—certainly not anything as good as a plaza in a lesser city like Barcelona, where you have a big square where the buildings define it like an outdoor room.

You can count on one hand the deliberately created public places in Manhattan that have any artistry to them. Gramercy Park is a lovely part of Manhattan, the little two-acre park there allows the buildings around it to be very grand and raises their real estate value. The thing is that it's a private park. When all's said and done, you need a key to get in there.

And there's Bryant Park, which is just a half a block of greenery behind the 42nd Street library. But there just isn't a lot there. The only thing you get in New York City is this massive Central Park of a thousand acres at the very center of it all, but you don't get much at all in the way of meaningful public space artfully designed anywhere else.

Contracting Cities

Duncan Crary: Jim, you don't think the skyscraper districts of our big cities are going to be successful in the future—they may not even be "successful" now in some ways. But you do believe American cities are going to have to contract in the future—the people and the businesses and the activities are going to return to more dense, traditional, walkable city centers.

James Howard Kunstler: I do think that all cities in North America—all major metroplexes, whether they're eastern ones or in the Sunbelt—I think they're all going to contract. This will be a global phenomenon—it won't just be in the US. We're seeing it first here because we pumped up the first industrial economy, after England, and we're the first to really flame out and tank. So the places

Frederick Law Olmsted

Olmsted is a very interesting character in American urban history. He is the great park maker. But he created a lot of mischief because Americans now only know one kind of park, and that's the big landscape simulation of the rural countryside that has been vanquished by the colossal new industrial city—that is what Central Park is.

The Olmsted Park is our main model for how to do parks in this country and consequently, our cities tend to have big parks and very few small ones that are distributed equally around the fabric of the city so that the city can really breathe.

There's also a problem with the conflict between romanticism and formalism, because the parks of Olmsted are based on this idea of trying to recapitulate the arbitrary way that nature does things. But you need more overt formality to make small parks work.

Formal parks don't contain much of an understory—the trees are there and the trunks of the trees are there, but mostly you can see between them. You can see the benches and things between them. You can see to the other side, generally, to the buildings, and there is no place for dangerous people to hide. That is one of the things that they do so well in Paris where they never abandon the idea of formality and geometry.

We do these small parks in America and we fill them up with arbitrary plantings of shrubs and hedges and things and then we are surprised that people regard them as dangerous.

—James Howard Kunstler, July 31, 2008
KunstlerCast #25: "Frederick Law Olmsted"

where that occurred—Detroit, Cleveland, Dayton, Toledo, Akron—these are the places that are really contracting very badly.

The question is how this contraction is going to occur and how we respond to it. We've got a tremendous job ahead of us in downscaling our cities and reforming them and de-automobilizing them. The amount of work that's going to involve is enormous. In fact, I hope it doesn't overwhelm us, and I hope we're able to do it.

DC: I've been reading about how Youngstown, Ohio, and Flint, Michigan are proactively making plans to shrink their cities.[3] These were cities that became pretty large during manufacturing boom periods. But now that the industries have moved away, there are a lot of abandoned and underactive parts of town. Things are pretty spread out now and the leaders are trying to redirect people and businesses back into a more compact, manageable area again.

JHK: What you can say about Flint is true of so many cities across the nation, particularly in the old rust belts in the Upper Midwest and here in the Mohawk and Hudson valleys. The condition is pretty similar, whether you're in Grand Rapids or Kalamazoo or Rock Island, Illinois, or Indianapolis—these are towns that are increasingly cored. There's less activity in the very first rings around the centers. And they're contracting. The city governments in Flint and Youngstown have come up with a kind of outright policy for managing the contraction. This involves taking over buildings and houses and knocking them down so that there's no longer any squatting and public safety issues.

The contraction process is very painful and highly visible, and it creates a lot of anxiety in us as we witness it occurring. We see all this property vanishing and disintegrating in the city centers. There's often a huge wish to rescue it, which is inconsistent with what the economy can provide or afford right now and it doesn't happen. So if a place like Flint, Michigan, is trying to manage its own contraction, that's something that we should probably applaud. It's a worthy effort to try to manage it. I hope they choose the things they really can manage and stay away from the things that are probably just going to get them in trouble.

Obviously Detroit is the mother ship of all the disintegrating Rust Belt cities, although it's not that much worse off than Cleveland. So this disease is pretty far gone and pronounced.

DC: The contraction is a little different in Detroit, because it's so much bigger than Youngstown and Flint— it's geographically larger than Manhattan, Boston and San Francisco combined. And it may contract into multiple urban villages.

JHK: The city officials of Detroit are going into whole urban areas and demolishing the residue of the ruined buildings because they want to deactivate the infrastructure—especially the water and sewer stuff that they don't want to pay to maintain now. They're sort of trying to preserve it in amber for what it is, but it'll probably rot out anyway.

We don't really know what the destiny of those neighborhoods is going to be. The whole region around Detroit may end up becoming a region of smaller urban organisms separated by stretches of some kind of agricultural land.

I remember going to Detroit in the late eighties and early nineties to do the legwork for a chapter in *The Geography of Nowhere*. Back then, the buildings were still there in what were then the slums around the old nineteenth-century neighborhoods. Seven years later they were wild-flower meadows.

DC: That's like the Talking Heads song "(Nothing But) Flowers."[4]

JHK: Now they're going through another iteration—they're becoming gardens. People are growing vegetables. There will probably be many other layers and cycles of this as we sort it out. We'll probably go from the situation where people are casually gardening a lot of empty vacant space to the point where people are building houses and cottages in and amongst these spaces. Sooner or later the centers of these towns will start to re-densify.

So much of it depends on emergent, self-organizing behavior that even under the best of circumstances you may not be able to plan. And I would advise against thinking it's normal for an urban area to be relabeled as a farm—because that's probably a typological mix-up. From my point of view, we need to remain aware that even as farming becomes a more local thing—and industrial agriculture winds down—the places that will be successful will be the places that have some agriculture near and around them. Under the best conditions that's going to happen on the fringe of town, in the place beyond the urban part.

I think we also have to remember that most cities are where they are because they occupy important sites. So something will probably be in most of these places, especially the cities in the Upper Midwest and the

Rust Belt, because most of them are located on waterways or important rail lines. The waterways aren't going away even if everything else does. So there'll be towns and settlements there. But they're not going to be the industrial-scaled, industrial-strength settlements that we've been used to in our lifetime.

City by City

DC: One of the complaints I hear from older folks is the idea that "America saved Europe during the war, then we 'rebuilt' their bombed-out cities." And somehow *that's* why European cities are OK now and US cities are in such bad shape.

JHK: It's one of those ironies of history, which seems to be a great prankster. It is ironic that we won the war and our cities look like we lost the war. They lost the war and their cities are now graceful, fully active, lively, wonderful, pleasant places.

DC: We could have rebuilt our cities after World War II, too. But we built suburban sprawl instead. We spent a lot of money making our own country look like we lost a war here.

JHK: In Europe, they made a totally different set of choices. They decided that they weren't going to throw their cities away—in fact, they were going to rebuild the ones that were badly damaged, even if they had to do it at the microscopic level. Warsaw and some of those Middle European cities and German cities that were just bombed to smithereens—they went back and they replaced the old buildings that were there before, brick by brick in many cases. There are whole neighborhoods where they replicated the fabric that had existed there.

It wasn't just an exercise in nostalgia—it was an exercise in recapturing their own culture and their own history. We have not been terribly interested in that. It's only really been since 1963, when we made the terrible blunder of knocking down Penn Station, that some people in America began to turn around and say, "Wow, we cannot destroy all of our history." After that, the historic preservation movement was born, and some people became sensitive to what was being lost. But it's still a terrible struggle. Every day there are still important, wonderful structures that could be reused and that are beautiful and that were designed with skills that we don't even have anymore.

I'm always amazed when I go to the Midwest and I see these towns whose names we all know from popular song and Broadway musicals—Rock City and all these old places—and there's nothing left. They've destroyed their town centers and many of their historic buildings and driven freeways through them.

One of the things I notice when I go down South is how little regard they have for their own history, and how they've allowed their towns and cities to commit suicide, and how destructive they are. It's comparable to the military mentality, which is a big thing down there, because the military has been such a big part of the local economy in many places there. So the destructive impulses that go along with militarism have gone along with the way that they develop the landscape. They heedlessly destroy things. They heedlessly destroy even the good stuff they have in the few cities that are historic.

I had a gig up in Peterborough, Ontario, Canada, and I decided to drive up there. My god, what a wild ride through the backwaters of farthest upstate New York, a place that's so battered and shuttered and shattered. Watertown, New York, just blew my mind. Our country is beginning to look like a third world nation in comparison to Canada, our neighbor to the north.

Favorite American Cities

DC: What are your favorite cities in America?

JHK: Well, there aren't a whole lot of them that are really wonderful. In fact, it's a very short list:

Portland, Oregon

Portland is really adorable by American standards. It's a *real* city. The scale is wonderful. They have very few buildings over ten stories, and yet, they have a wonderful cosmopolitan atmosphere within about a twenty-block area.

You feel like you're in an appealing, satisfying, rewarding place where you can have a life. Young Americans can imagine that the place would give something back to them. I imagine a lot of young Americans have grown up in suburbs and had their fill of it and don't want to go back to that sterile boredom of those empty streets and generic, stupid chain store restaurant things.

In Portland the physical accomplishments of progressivism in the civic setting are so visible in the excellence of the city compared to other American cities, and in the good choices they've made, that it's hard to assail them.

There are some schlocky townhouse things from the seventies and eighties that were not well conceived when they first started their experiments in densifying the city. But on the whole the newer stuff gets better, which is not the usual case in America.

A lot of land was lost, even inside the urban growth boundary, to worthless futureless suburban crap. However, they really did manage to defend the good farmland outside of town, and it will continue to be there.

Savannah, Georgia and Charleston, South Carolina

I'm very partial to Savannah, Georgia. It may be my favorite city in America, except for the weather. Living there is like living in a dog's mouth about five months out of the year.

Charleston, which is only about a hundred miles away, has a very different kind of building typology, equally wonderful and beautiful. Savannah's mostly nineteenth-century brick and Charleston is mostly eighteenth-century wooden, the best historic parts of it.

Both of these are historic cities that are very fully alive even though they're made of, more or less, antique city fabric.

Boston, Massachusetts

I've always liked Boston a lot. It's a fully activated city. There are a lot of people still living at the center. It's really alive. It, too, is way overwhelmed with automobile infrastructure and traffic and everything that goes with it. They're going to have to retreat from that, and they probably will.

New York City

I remain very fond of my hometown, New York City, although I'm not very bullish on its prospects. I think it's reached the point now where it is so severely overwhelmed with skyscrapers that I just don't see how it's going to make it in a post-fossil-fuel era.

Washington, D.C.

I've always kind of liked Washington, D.C., although it too is a very, very car-oriented place. I drove a cab there in 1975 after I quit *Rolling Stone* magazine. My first job after *Rolling Stone* was mopping floors in the National Portrait Gallery, and I did that for about three weeks and then I got a job driving a cab.

One of the great things about Washington is that it has a very harsh height restriction for its buildings.

City Flybys

James Howard Kunstler: The places that really fascinate me are the places where there's a collision between something closer to my sensibility and something that's that alien, Middle American, conservative, NASCAR, suburban mentality.

Boulder, Colorado

I see it most vividly in a place like Boulder, Colorado—where they're surrounded by these seas of tract houses and foreclosure estates, and a tremendous suburban sprawl clusterfuck of all the worst kind of crap that I've ever imagined. They've built a town that's about 93 percent suburban crapola, yet at the very core of this town are yuppie Boomer progressives.

Phoenix, Arizona

Phoenix is an unspeakable UFO landing strip that's totally out of control, beyond belief and probably beyond help. It has no future.

Flagstaff, Arizona

By American standards today, especially Western standards, Flagstaff is a fairly pleasant place…because it's not Phoenix. Flagstaff is much more manageable but it still shares the characteristics of most Western places in so far as there's very little pre-automobile fabric there. Most of the stuff there comes in the form of the strip mall or the pod or something like it. Unfortunately, most of Flagstaff, Arizona, looks like the

---

When JHK Comes to Town

Inviting provocative New Urbanism proponent James Howard Kunstler to your city is well-known to be an exercise in self-flagellation.…

The reason he stirs so much passion is perhaps even more obvious when he's doing his KunstlerCasts…than when he's on the lecture circuit.

Listening to these arch commentaries—even if you agree with him about bad sprawl and ugly skyscrapers—it's hard not to feel the curdling resentment of indigenous people under observation by pith-helmeted anthropologists.

—Journalist Fern Shen, April 11, 2010
"Kunstler touts some Baltimore neighborhoods, but trashes…Formstone?" *Baltimore Brew*

service road that surrounds Newark airport.

Arizona was one of the epicenters of the housing bubble implosion so I would say they're probably nearing the end of building out farther into the mountains there. They're going to have to face the consequences of that housing bubble, which is going to be pretty severe even in Flagstaff.

New Orleans, Louisiana

It's a lovely, charming, wonderful, memorable, rewarding, fabulous place. I think it's going to be a smaller city than it was in the late twentieth century. And it's not necessary for it to be that enormous anymore. It can be a fine, wonderful place at a smaller scale.

Baltimore, Maryland

When people think of Baltimore, they mostly think about that TV show *The Wire*, which portrays the whole city as a hopeless total ghetto. But that's just not the way it is.

It's half dead and half wonderful. In many ways it's a very damaged city. It's not in the same league with Detroit and it's better off than Cleveland. But there are some parts of it that are very interesting and fun and heartening. There are wonderful neighborhoods in working order. And there is a downtown business district.

There are a lot of wonderful neighborhoods within a mile of the absolute center of the inner harbor—like Federal Hill, Fells Point and Canton, etc. But you get beyond that three-quarter mile radius and then everything is toast.

I sometimes think of Baltimore as being the poster child for how cities are going to contract in this country. Baltimore was a great industrial town as well as being a harbor city and it too has undergone this pretty massive contraction.

But one way or another Baltimore is going to have to reinvent a local economy. If it's lucky it will. It does have the benefit and amenity of this fantastic harbor.

Minneapolis, Minnesota

The physical design in Minneapolis is pathetic compared to what they were able to accomplish in Portland during the same period of time.

There's definitely a lot about Minneapolis–St. Paul that's cool. But the downtown of Minneapolis is not cool. They've done one stupid thing after another and they persist in allowing these bad conditions to continue. The streets are typically six-laners with no on-street parking, so each one behaves like an expressway. They put up these gerbil-run skyway walkways all over the network of the downtown, so nobody's on the street. Everybody's up elevated on the second floor.

Sure it's cold there, but people also walk around the streets of Stockholm and Oslo and Moscow. You don't have to have skyways. That's a choice that people make.

The social scene is fine. The cultural scene is rich. But the downtown is a shitty downtown. I've been to the other neighborhoods that have their centers and their strips and they're OK. They have places that are sophisticated—they're not physically beautiful, but they have a lot of great programming. There are smart people there. There are industries that require people to think.

There's a lot to be said about Minneapolis aside from its physical design. But they've got to do better. Minneapolis is a city that's just not worthy of the programming and the people who are there.

Seattle, Washington

There are a lot of things about it that are appealing, but the scale is overwhelming.

San Francisco

I've made a couple of trips out to San Francisco over the last three years. One of the things I've been impressed with is what a heroic job of overlaying automobile infrastructure they've done over this city that's crammed into a rather limited peninsula sticking out into the ocean there on the West Coast.

San Francisco's got a pretty severe automobile overlay. There are features of it like Geary Boulevard, which is a freeway-like thing that cuts across the center of the city. The streets are generally too wide.

The cars generally go too fast. They could do a lot more to discipline the automobile than they've done.

Also, they made a big mistake in not keeping the cable car normal. By turning them into this tourist attraction, they've made it impossible for normal people to use them normally. They've got these little nineteenth-century cars that go "clang, clang" and everybody thinks, "Oh, it's so cute." Meanwhile, all the normal people who actually have to get up Nob Hill are stuck walking.

You could put another car on a parallel street and paint it battleship grey so the tourists don't think it's a cute conveyance and do it that way.

Los Angeles and Greater LA

Los Angeles in many ways is more urban and more dense than a lot of people realize. I would say Atlanta, Minneapolis and Dallas may be more purely suburban than Los Angeles.

But no mater what kind of buildings you're in—in what kind of neighborhood you're in—the car is still a part of the picture in Los Angeles. It's still a prosthetic extension of yourself and you have to lug it with you at all times and stash it wherever you are. The car culture in Los Angeles defines the experience of Los Angeles. It's such a composition of motoring infrastructure. That's what it's all about. Everything else seems incidental.

LA does have its virtues, but they're not that easy to get to. Even in the better districts you feel like everything is subordinated to cars being able to move around. If there were any fuel scarcity issues at all, that city would unravel and implode. So you get the feeling of this really provisional civilization out there that could just go up in a vapor at any moment.

West Hollywood

The quality of the streets is surprisingly charming there. But a stone's throw from the very urban blocks of West Hollywood you just go up the Hollywood hill and you're in one of those canyons and everything turns into a jungly suburb. Everything is just so discombobulated out there it's a wonder anyone can stay sane.

San Fernando Valley

It's supposedly the porn capital of the country. The hedonism out there in LA is palpable. You feel the hedonism pretty vividly. There's no question that there are so many perks and side benefits of being in show biz that are on the hedonistic side of the ledger that those too become pretty normal. And just being around people who are fit and beautiful day in and day out—and on the make—gives you a somewhat warped view of the world. There's definitely something sordid about it. But the people who are out there on the make are surprisingly hardworking.

Downtown LA

It's its own place. I think the truth of the matter is that if you actually work in the film industry and you were mostly based in Hollywood, you'd never have any reason to go down there and you wouldn't—maybe for years at a time.

They're just such separate worlds. The different worlds of LA are so very different. It's like a solar system made of different planets.

Santa Monica, California

It's pretty tight. It's got a lot of social cohesion. There are a lot of people who love Santa Monica for its civic qualities and its tightness and the fact that it has some sense of being an urban place. I'm not that crazy about it.

Cities of the New South: Atlanta, Georgia

The South did not have cities of consequence before air-conditioning. You're constantly aware of that when you go out of a building—that you've been in a denatured environment inside. And you've only been comfortable because you've been in an air-conditioned place.

Downtown Atlanta—there ain't nothing going on there except for a few huge monolithic buildings from the 1960s and '70s.

There are interesting things going on there in other parts of the city. But downtown is a horror. It's full of buildings that have blank walls facing the street and all sorts of weird concrete planters. You get these weird transitions of materials, because there's so much surface parking that you go from chain-link fence and razor wire to privet hedge to stucco and it's all blank.

You have to drive a car there to get anywhere. So all these apartment buildings have massive structured parking behind them. It's like every building has to have its parking twin.

Small Cities and Towns

Troy, New York

Duncan Crary: One of the reasons I moved to Troy, New York is that I saw it as a nice, manageable small city where I can have the benefits of living in an urban neighborhood, but I can get out into the country fairly easily; without driving, either.

I catch a fair amount of ribbing for not only living in Troy but for loving it. The suburbanites around here call it "the Troylet." And my

---

To Troy N.Y. Mayor Harry J. Tutunjian, On the Street:

This could be one of the great comeback cities in America if you play your cards right.

—James Howard Kunstler, December 18, 2008
KunstlerCast #43: "Missing Teeth in the Urban Fabric"

friends from New York City think I'm living in a backwater. But you're pretty sure that places like Troy are going to be where it's at in the future.

James Howard Kunstler: Troy is an interesting case, because it was so neglected for so long that it actually retained a tremendous amount of very valuable, pre-automobile-dependent fabric—great neighborhoods composed of really sturdy, brownstone row houses.

DC: They left about maybe 65 percent of the old city standing. Which is actually a lot compared to other places like it?

JHK: You bet. Troy has a tremendous amount of great buildings. In fact, part of the old downtown was so wonderful that Martin Scorsese went up there in the 1990s and used it as a set for his movie *The Age of Innocence*.[5]

DC: It's a small city, built for about 75,000 people. Now there are only about 45,000 residents, so we have a lot of deactivated buildings. What's left is pretty tight, right on the Hudson River. Believe it or not, there's one commercial shipping company headquartered here that still moves things along the Erie and Champlain canals and down the Hudson River.

We have some sprawl on the edge of town, but the transition from urban to rural is still rather abrupt. I imagine there are plenty of other small cities around the country in a similar situation.

JHK: You'd be surprised how different their circumstances are. Troy is an especially interesting case because its economy died so completely after about 1960, and so a lot of that suburban stuff just didn't happen on the outskirts.

There are some things that are fairly uniform. I get letters from people in towns all over America, their towns have been hit very hard economically, ever since the early seventies. And they're in terrible trouble, and they look bad, and they're failing economically. But the people who write to me live in these places, they love these places, and they care about them deeply. They have a deep interest in the revival of their life there. Even people like Chrissie Hynde, the lead singer of the Pretenders, came from Akron, Ohio—and went on this journey of celebrity and rock music, and moved to London and became a big star—she's now gone back to Akron, and she's got property there, and she opened a vegan restaurant there recently…

DC: She sings that great song that goes, "I went back to Ohio and my city was gone."[6]

JHK: "My city was gone…" Yeah,

that's right. It's interesting that we begin to hear those regrets and longings articulated in Generation X. They must feel that very strongly because it's been the background of their lives so vividly. So it's colored the lives of people who've come from that part of America.

These places are coming back, though. One of the reasons that they will is that in the future we're going to need human urban habitats that have a meaningful relationship with productive farmland outside of the city that's not three thousand miles away. We're going to need to grow a certain amount of our own food closer to home. In short, what had either already become suburbs or was slated to become more suburbs, that whole relationship is going to come to an end.

That's the other problem with the big metroplexes like Dallas, Atlanta,

New York City, Boston, Washington, etc.—they've so overgrown their agricultural hinterlands that their prospects for even feeding themselves are greatly reduced. People right now probably think that it's outlandish that I'm even suggesting this. But we're going to have a lot of trouble feeding the American population, and it's going to lead to very significant changes in the way the population occupies the landscape.

DC: Do you recommend that young people start to look to relocate to small cities like Troy?

JHK: I have a very different view of what's going to be happening to the big cities than many other commentators. I think that the big cities are going to be contracting substantially, and probably in a pretty disorderly way. They're going to enter insolvency, bankruptcy and difficulties in maintaining services. It's going to be pretty gnarly in the big metroplexes of America.

Personally I think the small cities and the small towns are going to tend to be the more successful areas. And young people ought to be very careful about choosing the places that they go. Part of that whole decision will be a regional decision. Do I move to Phoenix, Arizona, or do I move to the Northeast or to the Upper Midwest?

Places that are around water, that have good agricultural land—places that have small cities that exist at a scale that can be rebuilt—are all going to have advantages. The Upper Midwest now is a basket case, but it's also the center of the Great Lakes, which is the greatest freshwater inland sea in the world, and has tremendous possibilities at least for maritime trade on a regional basis. These are things that we're not thinking about at all yet, but they're going to come to play a much larger role in our society.

Reinvesting in small cities

DC: Do you have any thoughts on how small cities will be able to absorb increasing population influxes?

JHK: I've been thinking about this for quite a while because the area of the country that I've been in, for a long time, has been economically moribund for at least thirty years. Many of the cities here are small cities that have been deindustrialized and depopulated. But they're waiting to be reinhabited and reactivated.

I do think that we're going to see a very emphatic reversal of that two-hundred-year trend of people leaving the small cities and small towns for the big cities, and leaving the country places and the farms for the big cities. We're going to see a reversal of that because our big cities are simply not scaled to the energy diet of the future. We're going to have to downscale substantially. It's going to be a very difficult, messy process, and the people are going to go somewhere.

I think we're going to see a great demographic movement back to different living arrangements. We'll see people go back to the rural, agricultural landscape—occupying and inhabiting it in a different way than we've been used to. Instead of just one guy and a whole bunch of machines on twenty acres, we're going to need more people to work in the agricultural landscape. But the small towns and small cities are going to be reactivated, too, simply because they're much better scaled to the kind of energy situation that we're going to be in.

DC: Do you think there's any reason for the people who already live in these small, under-utilized cities to feel alarmed by the prospect of more people arriving in the future?

JHK: There already is cause for alarm because we've already had an interim population movement that people have been very disturbed by. We've seen a lot of what people call "welfare people" moving from New York City, Philadelphia and Boston into the smaller cities—they've become like Section 8 housing magnets for the poor.[7] So when people think about increasing the population now in these cities, all they think about is getting more poor people in there.

It's a disturbing picture because we need more than just poor people inhabiting our cities. We need people with a basic competency who can take care of themselves and do useful things. I do think that future waves will not necessarily just be desperate poor people. They may be desperate, but they may be desperate people who are educated, who really need to rearrange their lives in some way or another.

I'm actually very optimistic about the kind of small cities that we have been talking about.

DC: What kind of planning is involved to get ready for this?

JHK: It's certainly not just about infrastructure—it's not just about laying pipe or sewers, or more high-speed cable line, or any of that stuff. A lot of it has to do with changing what's in the regulations. For the most part, the norms and standards for any kind of redevelopment right now in most of America are still fundamentally suburban in the sense that even in the center city, there is far too much catering to the automobile and making provisions for the car—both in the street widths and the car storage issues.

Many cities in America, even the small ones, are hung up on structured parking. They will not allow apartment buildings unless there is a certain square footage of parking accompanying the building, or a structured parking building that is going to be allotted to the cars—for their cars to live in—and that's just crazy. That, by the way, is what you see in Atlanta—where they did make a heroic and sustained effort to urbanize midtown on Peachtree Street. But they made the huge mistake of requiring parking garages to accompany the midsized apartment buildings that were built. The parking garages are the same size as the apartment buildings. So it's a loony outcome, and only one that could have happened in the car-crazy Sunbelt.

City Murals

We put these murals on the blank walls of buildings, when, in fact, what we should do is enforce rules against blank walls, or infill the empty lots where the blank walls are exposed. Instead of encouraging that, we hire or engage amateurs, like schoolchildren, to paint these murals. And it's ridiculous. I've got a beef against murals, unless they're done with the greatest professional expertise.

—James Howard Kunstler, December 11, 2008
KunstlerCast #44: "Victorian Stroll"

We're also going to have to return to a much smaller increment of development. Right now, the increment of development is like a half a block, or several blocks. We're going to have to go back to the idea of the normal building lot, with a 25-foot frontage in the center of the city. That has ceased to be normal in our day-to-day habits and practices, and we're going to have to reinstitute that kind of traditional fabric.

Concentrating Poverty

Gentrification

Duncan Crary: I'm going to read you an email from one of our listeners and then I want to talk to you about the issue she raises in it:

> I listened to the latest podcast and I liked what you had to say about walkable cities. I just moved to Capitol Hill in Washington, D.C., and I love being able to walk to work, to the grocery store, and downtown. My neighborhood has wonderful sidewalks and fully-grown trees to shade us from that brutal D.C. July sun.
>
> My question is about something that has been on a lot of our minds here in our nation's capital: gentrification. As middle-class people like me move into neighborhoods like Capitol Hill—that are wonderful in part because they were overlooked by developers—what happens to the poor people that are being pushed out? If they move out to the suburbs, where it's become

cheaper to live, they have the extra burden of needing a car because there is no mass transit out there.
—Kara, in Washington, D.C.

James Howard Kunstler: It's a very complicated issue. I think we could start by making the point that it was never the norm in city life for cities to be inhabited mostly by poor people. That's a distortion and a perversity that has only occurred because of what we did in America, because all of the people who were doing well had the option of living in suburbia. The cities were left by default to everybody else, which were the people who weren't doing well in one way or another.

It's an abnormality in the first place that our cities are inhabited by so many poor people at the center. If you go to other cities in other lands, what you discover is for the most part the cities, at their centers, are inhabited by the people who are doing OK and the poorer people live in the periphery.

DC: Like in Paris.

JHK: Like in Paris. That's been the norm. Cities are not just for poor people. Cities have to be the responsibility of people of all classes but particularly the well-off, because if rich people can't take care of their towns, who can? We really find ourselves in a bind, where in order to get back to the original form of an urban habitat we have to allow people of all incomes to live in proximity to one another.

If you start creating rules and regulations against improving neighborhoods and against well-off people inhabiting the cities then you have to ask yourself: where do they go? And the answer is: they go to the suburbs. If it's morally not cool for them to fix up the neighborhoods in the center of the city, then they either have to go to the edge of the city or outside the city. It leaves us back in that predicament again.

I guess the question really is: what are the scale and quality and shape and character of our cities going to be like from here on? I would maintain that we have really gotten past the age of the industrial city, as we knew it. That is a story that's now coming to an end. I think the cities are going to be smaller, they are going to contract, they are going to densify at their centers. The people who are doing OK, if there are any in our society, will come to inhabit a lot of those places.

I don't know where the poor people are going to go. I don't know what the poor people are going to do. Right now, the poor people are doing a lot of things that are not necessarily productive for themselves. That's a whole other social issue that is maybe beyond the scope of what you and I are talking about. It's unfortunate that we have large populations that are poor and not doing well and seem to be stuck where they are. Those are social issues and social questions that may not be able to be addressed sheerly by physical form. Physical form can only do so much.

But there are things you can do. One thing is that, as neighborhoods are getting better in the cities, you can typologically make provision for people of different income levels to inhabit the same blocks or the same neighborhoods. You can do that by activating the dwellings in the alleyways and allowing them in the first place, allowing accessory apartments.

In many neighborhoods in America they have outlawed accessory apartments, meaning that families living in very large houses cannot assign part of the house to being rental space for someone who's not in the market for a single-family home— a single person, or an older person. That's the norm in other cities. We don't do that. We zone people out typologically.

DC: We hear a lot about gentrification battles in Washington, D.C., which has a substantial black population. Another city where we hear a lot of concerns about gentrification is New Orleans, where the majority of the population is also black. A lot of the concerns you hear about "gentrification" are really about racial issues. What are the underlying moral/racial issues that are occurring when people talk about their fear of gentrification? Do you think there are underlying racial guilt issues with gentrification?

JHK: Yes. A lot of it has to do with the failure of the social justice movement in the late twentieth century, and our embarrassment over the fact that we still have these large populations of one racial group that seem to be chronically unsuccessful and can't change their circumstances and get out of this predicament.

It's very hard to account for, and it embarrasses us and makes us tremendously uncomfortable. So we can't talk about it in those terms. But when you really get down to it, people are people. And it's a question of: What are you, Mr. Individual Person, going to do to take care of your life? If you're poor, if your family's poor— even if your family's been poor for three generations—are you going to make a decision to try to do everything possible to not be poor? Or are you just going to submit to where you are because somebody has convinced you that structural racism will prevent you from ever succeeding?

I'm not really sure where structural racism, so-called, leaves off and personal behavior issues begin. It's very important for us to have that discussion. And it's reassuring that Barack Obama started to touch on the edges of that discussion while running for president.

DC: When we talk about gentrification, should we make it a moral issue about race relations?

JHK: I would certainly say that we have to think about it in all of its dimensions.

"Urban" as a Euphemism for Black

DC: It's a strange thing, but there is this unhealthy evolution of language in our culture, where "urban" is code-speak for "black."

JHK: It's peculiar. But I think it's become the acceptable euphemism, for now. At some point it won't be, because it suggests that the center of the city is the only place that's suitable for black people, and that black people should be urban. The whole thing is crazy, especially when you consider the fact that many of the black people who ended up in the cities were former sharecroppers—country people—who moved to these cities to get jobs in the 1950s and '60s.

DC: It seems trivial to complain about the urban-means-black misnomer. But I can't help thinking that even this little sleight of language is part of what makes the whole issue of gentrification so touchy, and why it's hard to have an honest discussion about it.

JHK: Somehow we do have to talk about these things. And when we do, the best thing we can do is just try to remember to be kind to each other as much as possible.

Le Corbusier, Radiant City and the Projects

DC: What can you tell me about housing project towers? That's one building typology that we associate with urban poverty, the vertical housing projects.

JHK: They're all about concentrating poverty, which is never a good idea, and it was something we just didn't know at the time. They're in the spirit of Le Corbusier, or "Corbu" as he is sometimes called, the great troublemaker of the twentieth century. Charles-Édouard Jeanneret was his original name. He came out of Switzerland, moved to Paris and started to innovate the whole idea of the "Radiant City." He was the guy who wanted to knock down the Marais District on the right bank of the Seine in Paris and replace it with something that looks like Co-op City with a bunch of sixty-story mega-structures—all identical, all deployed in geometrical, absolutely regular lines with freeways servicing it and separated supposedly by park land.[8] This is in the middle of the city.

Corbu's plan was never carried out in Paris, although they did do some disastrous things right outside the city center. Once you get toward the edges you do start to get towers, and the slums of Paris are kind of done in that mold. But he was never allowed to knock down the center of the city, thank God.

Unfortunately, his influence persisted and he conjured up what ended up being the model for the housing projects of the United States. Right after the Second World War, we got busy doing the "Radiant City" all over the USA, and it took the form of housing for the poor. It ended up being the single, most influential pattern in urban design in the twentieth century. And wherever it landed it was a fiasco. Wherever we did the "Tower in the Park," it destroyed cities and city life.

Experimentation Upon the Poor

JHK: Interestingly, what you get is experimentation on the poor. We're taking these new untested forms of urbanism and trying them out on poor people. Rich people have the resources, so that if they don't like their habitation, they can just pick up and leave and buy something better or different. But when you're experimenting with the poor and you stick them in these experimental urbanist structures, they can't get out. So it ends up being rather cruel.

We stuck our poor in these places from the 1950s on, and beginning around the 1970s we started to have second thoughts. That was when one of the great iconic demolitions occurred, of the Pruitt-Igoe projects in St. Louis. They were sixteen years old when they were blown up. But they had so quickly fallen into a terrible social disorder that the people in St. Louis felt like they had to get rid of them.

What it came down to was this whole problem of concentrating poverty. It's one thing if you're going to have poverty in your society. It's another thing if you're going to ghettoize it and concentrate it all in one very small area. When you do that you tend to get really bad behavior.

I was very impressed when I went to Charleston, South Carolina, a few years ago to research a chapter for one of my earlier city books. Joseph Riley has been the mayor for a long time there. He had a very aggressive police chief too, and they got together. They understood that you can't concentrate poverty. They made a rule down there that you couldn't have more than eight units of subsidized housing in any given spot in the city. It ended up being a very good decision.

The Cycle of Poverty

JHK: But that was not the decision that was made in most other American cities, where we just concentrated the poverty. One of the consequences was that you got a lot of teen pregnancies and a lot of children who went on to become dysfunctional adults and to reproduce more. So it even promoted the replication of more criminal people and more and more dysfunctional people.

When the city is only composed of poor and struggling people, they become the only constituents for

the government. So you get another round of having to find some way to subsidize housing for them. That becomes a vicious circle. But my guess is that once you empty out the vertical slum, and the people who were there before disperse to other places, they won't really come back.

So it would be a mistake for us to think that cities are only for poor people, and that urban only means a certain ethnic group, and that our cities will never be something else. I think that they will be something else. I think that they'll be smaller, but they'll be finer, and that all the classes of people will be inhabiting the cities. There will also be people who are doing OK living in the cities. And if we're lucky, the people who are doing OK will feel responsible for the people who are not doing OK and maybe do a little bit more for them, a little bit better.

Handicap Access

There are an awful lot of things we do now that are contrary even to our wish to be inclusive. We create a lot of obstacles even beyond the obvious ones that make it difficult for people of different abilities to use the environment of everyday life. If you look at a traditional "Main Street" business district, the businesses and the shop fronts are all on grade with the sidewalk. There was never any question that if you were in a wheelchair or on crutches you could get into the store. And everything you needed in your life was within a quarter mile.

Now, 98 percent of the new commercial stuff that was built after 1960 was built in malls, and strip malls, and power centers, and places that you need a car to travel to. I don't imagine that makes life a whole lot easier for people who have difficulty getting around or require wheelchairs.

—James Howard Kunstler, July 10, 2008
KunstlerCast #22: "Handicap Access"

Anti-Urban Bias

Duncan Crary: I've noticed something strange going on in the "inner city," in the ghetto neighborhoods. The public housing projects that the City of Albany, for example, is putting up are practically suburban condos. They don't look or act like urban buildings. It's the suburbs plunked in the middle of an urban neighborhood that has no amenities left. These people are essentially trapped in suburbia...in the middle of the city.

James Howard Kunstler: I've seen that around the country. It's a very retrograde kind of behavior. In many cases, the only mental picture that the community development people have of a prosperous part of America that works is the suburban part. So what they are doing is they're taking typologically suburban buildings and they're plopping them in the urban setting where they really are inappropriate.

I saw a lot of this in Cleveland in the nineties when I was going back and forth there—they were very aggressively planting ranch houses where there used to be three- and four-story row houses from the 1870s that had become slums. There is an unfortunate tendency for public housing to take on a more and more suburban character and then to be joined by the other suburban accessories—the one-story strip mall. That's a real missed opportunity to build the kind of affordable housing that is found everywhere else in the world except the United States: the apartment over the store.

By the way, people live like that in Paris and London and they don't feel like they are being punished. Very wealthy people live in apartments on the third floor, over a delicatessen or a pork store or a bakery. And it does not diminish the quality of their lives. In some cases the quality of their lives improves because they can go right downstairs and buy a fresh croissant and take it up to their apartment. But in America, we had the chance to do it that way and we just blew it.

DC: I live in an apartment above

a business in a wonderful little urban business district. Some of the suburban people I know think I'm living in a ghetto, though. Sometimes I think they have such an anti-urban bias programmed into them that they just assume that if the buildings are connected and have some sort of mixed use, then it must be "the ghetto."

JHK: In the American version, both of these neighborhoods are probably deficient. The urban neighborhoods are not good enough and the suburban neighborhoods have structural deficiencies of their own that are self-evident. There are many ways of understanding the deficiencies of the suburbs. But the cities themselves in the USA have very few examples of true city life that are appealing. There are little pockets here and

---

Car Cops

I've got to think that in the police departments—given the kinds of people who become police and how police departments are run—there must be huge resistance to getting out of the car. Just like any suburban situation where once the car becomes normal you can't drag people out of it.

So what you get is law enforcement only taking place on the highway scale, or the road scale, not on the sidewalk scale. But when all is said and done, they're probably much more effective on the beat.

—James Howard Kunstler, April 16, 2009
KunstlerCast #60: "Bad Behavior"

there, like parts of Charleston and parts of Savannah—every city in America has at least one pretty good neighborhood left. Columbus, Ohio, has a couple of good neighborhoods. My favorite is called German Village, which is a neighborhood of gable-ended houses. It dates from about the 1850s, I think. Pretty wonderful.

But there's not enough of this around America that's in good shape—so the people can feel that what is good is anything but an elite ghetto for rich people in the city. There certainly aren't enough normal, middle-class neighborhoods that have the same kind of amenities. We're doing such a poor job with the urban set-ting in America and we'll continue to for quite a while, even when the automobile age gets into big trouble. And it's going to take a long time to hash it out.

DC: I find myself constantly trying to bite my tongue around suburbanites. They seem to have no problem telling me I live in a ghetto. But they're extremely defensive about their cul-de-sac or development.

JHK: The way we live in America now is so perverse at every end of the spectrum that neither side is going to appreciate the other side's argument. Frankly, I can understand why some people would make the suburban choice.

——— Missing Teeth in the Urban Fabric ———

Duncan Crary: There's a novelist who went by the pen name "Trevanian" who described the row house where he grew up in Albany as looking like "An old gentlewoman with her front teeth knocked out in a bar brawl."[9]

I get that same feeling looking at the entire block where I live in Troy. The neighborhood at-large is fairly intact, with buildings lining both sides of most streets. But on my particular block, we have a parking lot right across from my apartment and another parking lot directly behind. So I look at this streetscape and it looks like a Victorian lady got her teeth knocked out in a bar brawl. There are a few "missing teeth" in the urban fabric.

James Howard Kunstler: That's exactly what we call them, "missing teeth."

DC: I guess it's convenient for people going to the concert hall on the next street over, but that parking lot kills my block. It makes the whole street look uninviting and it discourages you from walking down it. When I'm walking on a city street where all the buildings are connected and there aren't any vacant lots or missing teeth, I feel good about the progress I'm making with each block. It's a psychological thing.

JHK: Absolutely. The urban designers that I know and respect are very keenly aware of it. And they call it the missing tooth problem. There have been guys out there, like William "Holly" Whyte, who was a writer on urban behavior back in the sixties and seventies and ran a graduate program at Columbia University. Whyte and people like him—Fred Kent—have studied this and they know that missing teeth on streets repel people. People will cross the street rather than continue walking on the side where the empty space is.

Parking Militants

DC: The thing about these missing teeth is that many of our city leaders, whether they're politicians or business owners—they always want more parking, which just creates more missing teeth.

JHK: It's amazing how that evolved over the years. Obviously, it goes hand in hand with unbelievably extreme car dependency. You could put half of Sienna, Italy, in some of these so-called urban renewal districts. But an interesting thing happened. These districts never underwent urban renewal, at least not for a very long time, because what happened after the destruction of the neighborhoods and the blocks is that the citizens in town discovered that they actually valued the property more for car storage than for urban activities—like buildings and businesses and apartments and things to do and places to live and theaters or anything else you might have in a city. All of that was valued less than your ability to stash a car somewhere.

It had the strange consequence in my little town, Saratoga Springs, of turning a small American town that had some dimension to its center into little more than a main street corridor. The business district, which had once covered multiple blocks, had been reduced to just this one corridor with these wastelands of parking on either side. It's been getting infilled, but there's still quite a bit of the parking left. That's really what the big battle is over—should we continue to infill it or should we keep the parking? For the moment, the parking is prevailing. Even progressive politicians have taken a stand against further downtown renovation and infill. Why? Because they feel that, once again, parking is a higher and greater use than buildings. The competition and tension and conflict between those two things is enormous. Even among the supposedly politically progressive people, parking wins.

DC: There are community leaders in my city who adamantly believe that people aren't coming to Troy because there isn't enough parking. But the thing is, no one goes to any downtown for the parking lots—whether it's Saratoga, or Burlington, or Columbus. They go for the attractions, the buildings. If there's something downtown that they want to get to, they will get there. If there's nothing to attract them down there, they won't go.

JHK: The New Urbanists themselves have, for years, made the point that the best places in the world are the places that are the hardest to drive around. You go to Perugia in Italy, a wonderful town, and you actually have to park outside of the town and either walk in or they have a very strange escalator system that you can take up to an elevated butte where the town really exists. Or in Sienna, Italy, you *can* take the car in—I once did it. But getting around in a car and then having to stash it is just madness. And you never want to see the fucking thing again while you're there.

The Jevons Paradox of Parking

DC: The other thing about providing lots and lots of free parking in cities is that you just end up creating more demand for more parking. It may be an example of the Jevons paradox.[10] Because when all your buildings are surrounded by parking, they become too far apart to comfortably walk between. People end up driving from parking lot to parking lot to get to their next destination. So you don't just need the parking to accommodate all the cars in your city at one time, you need the parking for four, five, eight times the number of cars because each car needs access to eight parking spots throughout the day.

JHK: Yes, and you're describing a self-reinforcing feedback loop, which starts with a problem and then ends up generating more of its own problem as it goes along.

DC: Another thing I don't get is that suburbanites who drive to the mall often have to walk three times the distance from their parking spot in the parking lot in front of the mall than they would in a normal downtown shopping district. But they complain endlessly about the parking in any urban area. They demand that they be able to park directly in front of the store if it's in an urban setting. You can't even do that at the mall.

JHK: I suppose it's some kind of a lizard brain homing instinct that's not all that rational. You're just programmed to try to get as close to your destination as possible.

How Real Estate Taxes Prevent Good Urbanism

DC: Why is it so hard to convince people of the value of urban infill— of erecting buildings with stores and cafés and apartments in the spaces that are now just parking lots and missing teeth?

JHK: Partly, it has to do with our real estate laws. I wrote a chapter in my 1996 book *Home From Nowhere* called "A Mercifully Brief Chapter On A Frightening, Tedious, But Important Subject," which was real estate taxes. I had been consorting with a group of people who followed the philosophy of Henry George, a nineteenth-century political reformer who focused a lot of his activity on tax reform. What he wanted to do was change the real estate taxing system so that we would levy taxes on the site value of the property rather than the improvements or buildings that you put on it.

I know this sounds very abstruse, but the way we tax things in our system today, you are actually penalized for putting up a good building. There's a tremendous incentive to put up the worst kind of building possible with the fewest uses—the least ability to generate rents or value out of it—because the better the building is, the higher your real estate taxes.

Under the Henry George system, you would be taxed on the basis of how close your property was to the center of things—the center of town, the center of the business district— how valuable the site was itself. It wouldn't matter whether you put up a crappy one-story packing crate or a magnificent five-story palazzo, or an even more magnificent building like the Troy Savings Bank Music Hall. They would all be taxed the same. So you would have a huge incentive to put up a magnificent building.

DC: That Henry George taxing system doesn't work when you have cars and cheap gasoline though, right? I imagine it might start to work again if the cost of everything keeps going up again.

JHK: Right. So, you start with this real estate tax problem and then you add on top of that the problem that we value surface parking so highly in our very unbalanced social scale of values that it makes it almost impossible to infill our cities. This city where you live—Troy, New York— has been so fortunate in as much as it has had so few demolitions. But you go to a normal American city like Dayton, Ohio, or Kansas City, or

Des Moines, Iowa…these places are like people with just one tooth in their head! There ain't nothin' left in the center but surface parking. Columbus, Ohio, which I've been to at least half a dozen times in the last decade—it's like 70 percent surface parking! They've done a magnificent job of destroying most of the fabric of the town with surface parking.

Now one way you can think about surface parking is that it's a form of land banking—at least there's nothing on it. The cars can be rolled off at some point and you can build something there.

To Build a Better Parking Garage

DC: So what's your take on parking structures versus surface parking lots? Which are more useful for cities now?

JHK: You could make the argument that it's better to stack the cars up in a five-story building. But I would maintain that continuing to build parking decks is just an enormous waste of whatever dwindling resources we have.

DC: But when you are building a parking garage, how do you build one that has the most benefit to the city with the least disruption?

JHK: These are bad investments because the future's not going to be about parking. But let's say hypothetically during the period where it seemed like a good thing to do—like maybe the early 1990s—you would want to at least line the ground floor with some retail so it has a relationship with the street that is more or less like a normal building, so it provides some destinations for people who are walking around town, gives people something to look at as they're traversing the block.

DC: One of the things I've heard you point out is that it's difficult to retrofit a parking garage, the way they're normally built, because the ceilings are too low to ever turn them into decent offices or apartments.

JHK: When you're building something other than a parking deck, you need some room overhead to run the ductwork and the plumbing and the service lines and all that stuff. So you have to have more than a seven-foot ceiling. The trouble with these parking decks is that they have fairly low ceilings that don't lend themselves to be retrofitted.

Also, there's the problem of needing a central light well. In a structure that large, if you were going to turn it into offices or apartments, you'd have to have a core in the center that would be a light well that would allow you to get light in from the outside to the apartments or offices that are more toward the center of the structure.

DC: You couldn't even use these things for warehouses. The ceilings aren't even tall enough.

JHK: Well, it would be a warehouse with very short floors.

DC: Have you ever actually seen a parking garage that was lined with retail and had taller ceilings and…?

JHK: Not taller ceilings. But the city of Charleston had a very successful program in the eighties and nineties under their wonderful mayor Joe Riley, who's been mayor for like thirty-five years there and is among the few elected officials in America who actually has a firm grounding in the particulars of design. They built a bunch of parking decks in downtown Charleston, but they took pains to make provision for retail on the first floor. I believe I saw something like that in Savannah, too. They're around the country.

Ridicule, Oppose, Accept

DC: But at this point you feel like even those better parking garages are a bad investment in the future. We shouldn't worry too much about luring suburbanites in their cars to spend money in our cities.

JHK: I do believe we will soon emerge to the point where it's self-evident that we shouldn't fill our cities with surface parking or structures for parking, because it'll be self-evident that the future is not about motoring. People will get it, and they'll get it very suddenly. And they won't even notice that nine months earlier they thought that motoring was going to be the determining factor in how we did everything.

One day they'll wake up with a

Diagonal Parking

In the early part of the Automobile Age, we had diagonal parking on the street. You can actually get a lot more cars parked that way. The trouble is, it cuts down on the travel lanes. It may actually be a much better strategy to net down the street and have the cars go slower. All in all, I think diagonal parking would probably be a better thing. But since we're sort of at the end of the Automobile Age, I kinda don't give a shit anymore.

—James Howard Kunstler, July 17, 2008
KunstlerCast #23: "One City Block"

different idea because it'll be obvious, and there will be something about the hive mind—the collective termite consciousness of mankind and its North American version—where they'll get it. This idea will spread with the force of a powerful subconscious meme. And everybody will realize, "Oh, yeah, that's right, we don't need that parking anymore because we're doing things differently now."

A Drugstore on Every Corner

Duncan Crary: The national chains and the fast food franchises tend to be very destructive in most American cities because they insist on doing business in a suburban manner—with one-story buildings, parking lots, drive-thru windows. The drugstore companies in particular seem hell-bent on knocking down perfectly good urban buildings to make room for their own little box. But something happens when people try to stop this kind of behavior—they end up making it a fight about how the chain stores are hurting the mom and pop stores. And the opponents will try to block the chain store from coming to town, which is usually a losing battle. You approach the situation differently.

James Howard Kunstler: There are two different issues here, which people are very confused about. One is the "programming," which is the business. The other is the "container" that the programming is in. You can go to plenty of other places in the world where they have wonderful buildings that contain this programming. It doesn't bother anybody. Nobody complains when the programming goes in the container, or building—before there was a drugstore in that building, there was something else.

Now, because we live in a throwaway culture in America, it's more convenient for these big chains to just tear down whatever is there and put up their own special purpose-built box with all of the things in the right place so that the building is sort of a pre-programmed machine for dispensing goods.

DC: These companies don't want to rehab old buildings because they can't put their aisle of candy bars exactly where they want, to maximize our psychology to buy this crap.

JHK: Yeah, if there's a wonderful historic building that has 9,000 square feet of space and the drugstore needs 9,402 square feet of space, they'd rather knock down the historic building just to get exactly the right amount of space.

DC: So instead of making it a fight about the chain store coming to town, how should we approach the issue?

JHK: A few years ago we were getting a lot of substantial new downtown infill buildings in Saratoga Springs and lot of people were complaining that the new tenants were the Gap or Eddie Bauer. What I told them about that was, "Don't worry about the programming on the first floor. What you got to worry about is the quality of the building." Because time will go by, the decades will go by, and those chain stores will leave—they won't be there anymore. Then something else will be there, possibly even a locally owned store, because our economy will be changing.

The national chains themselves are going to start running into very serious trouble with their business equations—with their huge continental supply lines and getting all their merchandise from twelve thousand miles away, and the just-in-time inventory system that depends on the incessant circulation of tractor-trailer trucks all around the country.

So the whole system of doing this is going to change. By necessity, we'll have to construct these more local and regional networks of commerce, and things won't be coming from so far away.

Last-Ditch Adaptive Reuse

Adaptive reuse is a wonderful thing. It's one of the reasons that the great European cities are so rewarding to be in, because you see these old buildings given new life repeatedly, and then they're wonderful to be around and among. In our country and our culture, sometimes it's all we can do to just save the facade. But that may be a good save because that's the public face of the building and that's its interface with the street and with the public realm, and I think it's important to do that. I'm actually glad they're saving these facades. I think of it as last-ditch adaptive reuse.

—James Howard Kunstler, June 11, 2009
KunstlerCast #68: "Historic Preservation"

Chapter 7: Urban Polemicists

Jane Jacobs

Duncan Crary: How do you feel about being compared to Jane Jacobs, and what kind of influence did she have on your writing and thinking?

James Howard Kunstler: We obviously have a lot in common. Mostly, I think what that's about is we were both polemical writers—writers who were intent on making a persuasive case for something and advocating for something relatively similar: the case for better urban life.

I think where we depart is that she was a very lonely figure profes-

sionally in her heyday, when she published her opus magnum, *The Death and Life of Great American Cities*, because there were very few people in the USA who were thinking coherently about these things in 1961. She didn't have very many allies, whereas I came along with *The Geography of Nowhere* in 1993 as the New Urbanist people were getting together. In fact, there was kind of a synchronicity about it because they formed their organization, the Congress for the New Urbanism, in the same year that

The Public Realm

The whole issue of satisfaction in our living places has to do with this thing called the public realm: the part of our world that belongs to everybody, that everybody ought to have access to most of the time. In America it comes mostly in the form of the street—'cause there's no residue of the Renaissance. We don't have medieval market squares. We don't have cathedral squares. We don't have that stuff.

In America we have some New England greens and courthouse squares in the Midwest and the South. But for the most part in the USA, public space comes in the form of the street and if you screw it up—if you dishonor it, if you fail to embellish it in a way that honors people's existence—then you've got a real problem. Having turned all our streets into automobile slums, we no longer have any sense that it is a public space and that it does belong to us. Certainly not that it honors us.

We're going to have to rediscover that. And by the way, it's not abstract. There's a direct relationship between people's satisfaction in a public place and the successful definition of space...using the walls of the buildings to function like the walls of an outdoor public room. You would no more put up a bad building or decorate it badly, or fail to embellish it, than you would have a bad wall in your own house that was full of graffiti or junk or careless nothing.

—James Howard Kunstler, April 28, 2011
KunstlerCast #154: "Q&A with JHK"
at The Sanctuary for Independent Media

I published *The Geography of Nowhere*. So there was a ready-made cohort, a club of people to hang out with, and there were scores of them—good people who were good thinkers. So I got a lot of support right away for what I was saying, whereas with Jane Jacobs, I think it was a continual uphill battle for her.

Jane Jacobs and Barack Obama

DC: It was interesting that during his presidential campaign, then Senator Barack Obama mentioned reading *The Death and Life of Great American Cities* and what an influential book it is. I don't know how many other presidents have ever mentioned Jane Jacobs.[1]

JHK: I'd be surprised if any of them besides Barack read her. I reread that book a few years ago before I went to interview her in Toronto and one of the things I rediscovered was that she was a wonderful writer.[2] It was a pleasure to read, as well as being very illuminating.

Jane Jacobs versus Robert Moses

JHK: Jane Jacobs started introducing ideas that people weren't thinking about much, that didn't have to do with design per se. One of her biggies was "Eyes on the Street." That idea is that when people are present— either on the sidewalks themselves or on the stoops of the row houses, or coming and going, or looking out the windows, or occupying the storefronts—when people are present then the city fabric is self-policing, and bad behavior tends to be suppressed.

She also engaged in a great battle, an epic struggle with the great diabolical figure of urban destruction, Robert Moses. She was his chief antagonist. Moses had done many things over the previous thirty-odd years that created a lot of mischief in New York City—with building the Cross Bronx Expressway and a lot of other roads. He was aiming to run a four-lane expressway across Greenwich Village, right through Washington Square Park. The whole thing would have been an obvious catastrophe. Jane Jacobs marshaled the community spirit in lower Manhattan to oppose this plan. Robert Moses was not used to being opposed, and he had never really been successfully opposed for any of the projects that he did. She started this battle with him, and she won. So it made her a great hero.

DC: How did she win this battle?

JHK: Through the public process and through whatever the planning board approval and permission process was in New York City. It was kind of the turning point for Robert Moses. It was the point where people realized, "Oh, this guy isn't the omnipotent Devil-like figure that we've been battling all these years. He can actually be disciplined." It wasn't too long after that that his power started to really wane.

So she began to give this rapidly suburbanizing nation, this nation that was no longer investing in cities and had lost interest in cities—she started to revive the interest in them and to give people some hope that they could actually be OK. American cities were very un-OK by the early 1960s. Not only had they been neglected during the Great Depression (and then not really taken care of very well during the Second World War either), but as soon as we emerged from the war, all of the resources in the USA were going into building suburbs. So the cities, which had never been really that great to begin with in America, just didn't get attention, didn't get resources. Everything that was done in them tended to be utilitarian and not very beautiful.

When we built a structure it was as cheap as possible, strictly to do the job that it had to do. Whatever it was—a skating rink or a municipal building—they all looked terrible. The cities were losing population and losing resources, and they were not very nice places to live. Jane Jacobs started this battle, which was still going to be a losing battle for a long time to come. It's a battle that still hasn't been won, although we've come back quite a ways from there.

Jacobs and Toronto

DC: Tell me a little bit about meeting her up in Toronto. What was that experience like?

JHK: First, I should tell the story of why she landed in Toronto. She was,

after all, the quintessential Greenwich Village New York Bohemian gal—although she originally came from Scranton, Pennsylvania, where her daddy was a doctor.

She got married, had kids, and by the sixties her kids were starting to grow up and become of the age of getting drafted into the army during the Vietnam War. So she and her husband packed up and took their kids out of New York and moved to Toronto to be out of the reach of the draft. She became quite an activist figure in the Toronto urban politics scene after that. I think it took her a few years to get some traction as being someone who was committed to being there for a long period of time.

But Toronto was also growing hugely. They had a huge immigration in Canada in those years, and the city was moving from being a fairly small place by US standards to becoming a major global city. So she was involved in all the controversies that were coming out of Toronto's growth. It was growing quickly, and in ways that weren't all that promising. The usual kind of suburban things were going on, although there are different ground rules in Canada. One of the important ones is that there's no income tax deduction for mortgage interest in Canada. That's important, because it puts renters and homeowners on the same footing in terms of taxes.

In the USA, people who are homeowners enjoy quite a tax advantage from being able to deduct their mortgage interest, and most of people's payments nowadays are the interest. So if you're paying a thousand bucks a month in a mortgage payment, most of it's interest and only a little of it is principal, and it's all tax deductible. In Canada that's not the case. People who rent apartments are not at a disadvantage, and consequently, more people live in the center of the Canadian cities. They still have their suburbs and they're still huge, but it's not quite as big a problem.

DC: How different is Toronto from New York City?

JHK: I don't think that it is that much different in character or from the feel of it. The main difference is that there are a lot more middle-class neighborhoods near the center. You get the feeling that city life there is not just for wealthy people and never was just for wealthy people. They never went through that traumatic change. There was always something normal about having normal people living near the center.

Meeting Jane Jacobs

DC: What kind of a place was she living in when you met up with her?

JHK: She lived in a single-family house in a very tight neighborhood where the houses were large and generous. They weren't grand, but they were decent size. They were pretty close together, and not far from the center of town. As I recall, she was living just off Yonge Street, which is one of the main drags there off of the downtown. It was a brick house on a tree-shaded street. Her kids were all grown up. Her husband had died—she was a widow living there alone.

The furnishings of her house were interesting because there were a lot of the, shall we say, incunabula of Bohemianism from the 1950s and '60s—all these kinds of primitive art and folk sculpture and stuff that I recognized from New York of the beatnik days. It was greatly nostalgic for me to see it.

DC: What was it like meeting her?

JHK: I had a lot of trouble with her actually answering the questions that I had prepared. A lot of it had to do with Long Emergency issues, and how the cities were going to respond to the global energy problems that were developing, and the implications for how we inhabited the landscape. She sort of didn't want to talk about that stuff. Really, what she wanted to do was drink beer and to just kind of banter.

It was easier to get her to talk about her past. By this time she was over eighty years old. She was rattling around this fairly big house like a BB in a packing crate all by herself. She took me up to her writing room, which was a very modest little spare room. She was writing on a typewriter, if I remember. Mostly she wanted to drink beer that day— not in the sense she was hooking down one after another, but she was enjoying them and she wanted me to do that with her. I'm not much of a beer drinker, so I couldn't really keep up with her.

DC: Jane Jacobs drank you under the table, Jim, is that what you're saying?

JHK: No, not really, we weren't under the table. But I couldn't really keep up with her. The funny thing was I was asking her all these Long Emergency questions about energy, and technology, and what we were going to do, and how things were not looking too great for advanced civilization and everything. And I didn't realize it at the time—because she didn't tell me what she was working on—but she was writing a book published under the title *Dark Age Ahead*. She was pretty much concerned with a lot of the same things that I was, only she didn't want to talk about them. I don't know, maybe they depressed her or something. But she sort of nailed it herself and she could see it coming from a million miles away.

DC: Maybe she didn't want you to scoop her.

JHK: Maybe. I wasn't writing *The Long Emergency* yet, but I was thinking about those things. I think at the time I was writing *The City in Mind*. I would still have a novel ahead of me before I did *The Long Emergency*.

She did have her wits totally about her. She knew what was going on. She wasn't the least bit senile, although, obviously, most of her life was behind her and her family was gone, dispersed to the four winds or passed away. So she was putting in her time in her last years in a worthwhile way. At the same time, she had become a great lady of Toronto and was still very involved in all the civic issues.

Lewis Mumford

Duncan Crary: You said Jane Jacobs was a lonely figure in her time, with few intellectual allies. There was one figure during that era who was at least challenging some of the tenets of suburbia: Lewis Mumford.

James Howard Kunstler: Mumford was another polemical writer, like Jane Jacobs. He produced such great prose, and he combined that with a very deep understanding of his subject matter, which was not just cities but the whole issue of technology generally, which he was obsessed with.

He was born at the very beginning of the twentieth century and lived through most of the whole thing. He lived to a very ripe old age, into his nineties, and he saw the whole cavalcade of technology and the whole rise of all the things we're familiar with like cars and planes and television and all the things that made suburbia possible. He understood—as few did along the way—its diminishing returns, its disadvantages, the unintended consequences.

He wrote about this at great length during a period when people didn't care much about it, because, for the most part, during the twentieth century most people just enjoyed that stuff and were unaware of the blowback. He understood the import of the General Motors Futurama exhibit at the 1939 World's Fair.[3] He understood how economic opportunists would want to take that idea and turn it into fortunes for themselves, at the same time that they destroyed American cities. Mumford was all over that, and he understood it, and he articulated it in a way that was savvy.

So you get to 1961 and by a weird coincidence he publishes his great magnum opus, *The City in History*, in the same year that Jane Jacobs produced *The Death and Life of Great American Cities*. In *The City*, Mumford writes long chapters about suburbia and the dangers of it and the huge liability that it's going to be for American society in the years ahead—this is when we're all getting shoehorned comfortably in the split levels, and the expressways were new, and "It's All Good" for suburbia. I have a feeling that he was regarded as a bit of a crank for this, or at least, let's say, never really sufficiently acknowledged or rewarded for saying what he did. But he said it beautifully.

He's got this one line that I quoted in *The Geography of Nowhere*, where he's talking about suburbanites at night sitting "in the cabin of darkness" in front of the boob screen.[4] He really got it, vividly, about where we were heading with the burbs.

DC: He had some other funny phrases too, like, "Our national flower is the concrete cloverleaf."

JHK: Yeah, the on-ramps and the off-ramps. That was a great line.

DC: And he knew Jane Jacobs personally?

JHK: He and Jane Jacobs were friends for a while. But then they had a big falling-out. I think that had to do with Mumford's body of ideas, where he really couldn't shake off the notion that the traditional city was a bad thing in some way.

Mumford grew up in Manhattan, and was really a creature of New York City through the whole twentieth century. So he saw some of the worst of city life, including the great tenements of the day on the Lower East Side. But I think his arguments were corrupted by some of the fashions *du jour*—the utopian Garden City experiments, which had many elements of the Bauhaus to it. The idea was that American cities were so dark and dingy and lightless and unsanitary, that the first priority was providing people with fresh air and light and plumbing, and a little bit of grass around them. But the trouble is, when you carry decongestion too far, you end up deurbanizing a place and you don't get the density or the mixed use that you need for a city to function.

A lot of these guys were so traumatized by the tribulation of these two world wars, that what was still very much on their mind was purging all of the awful claptrap of history out of society. They didn't want it anymore because they felt that it had been responsible for all of the trauma of the twentieth century, which was like nothing that had ever been seen before, and they wanted to purify the world. It wasn't just Walter Gropius and Corbu and the other real modernist architects. It was a meme that ran through the culture.

Robert Moses

He was sort of a hostage of his time. However good or bad or evil or whatever we think about him, he was really following the dictates of the circumstances that he was born into. He came up with the Age of the Automobile, and he served it loyally.

—James Howard Kunstler, October 8, 2009
KunstlerCast #83: "Jane Jacobs"

Chapter 8: Parting Words

Packin' for France

Duncan Crary: Do you think it's time to leave America, to get out of the US?

James Howard Kunstler: If I were a twenty-five-year-old with a lot of my life ahead of me, I would give some serious thought to maybe going somewhere else. I think apropos of all the town meeting uproars that have been going on over the health care debate and the really surprising ugliness that is emanating from those things—including a lot of really vulgar, hyper-patriotic

nonsense—the question of whether the US is headed for trouble is not necessarily identical to the question of, "Should I go somewhere else?" Or, at least, let's say there's a lot that you could talk about just on one side of the issue: what is going on in the US? Where are we headed? What's the timeframe for all that?

The question whether one can successfully be transplanted, that's a whole other thing. Back in the days when I was writing books about the New Urbanism and the fiasco of suburbia, my motto for a few years was, "There's always France." Because I'd go to Europe, and I'd see at least how the physical disposition of things and cities and towns was so far superior to the US, for the most part—granted there are some suburbs in these places, but on the whole it was superior. You land back in this slum airport of New York, and you want to cut your throat after returning from Europe.

DC: Why didn't you just hightail it to Europe right then? Why did you stay in this country?

JHK: There are a couple of reasons for that. When I first started pursuing these issues in *The Geography of Nowhere*, I'd never been to Europe. I was still pretty much a starving Bohemian. I didn't have two nickels to rub together. So it never occurred to me. Another thing was, I'm not very good at foreign languages. I took Spanish in high school and college, and I can just communicate enough to be a tourist in Mexico. But I can't speak French, other than asking, "What's on the menu?" or, "Please give me the bill."

And when I did end up going to France, where I've been many times since then, I always sort of floundered around there with the language. In fact, I got into the habit of just speaking English to them in a French accent, which seemed to work. They seemed to understand what I was saying. I never took that any further.

DC: If I just speak English slower and louder...

JHK: Right. So I was daunted by the language thing. Also in some ways I identify myself as kind of a true-blue American, but not in a dumb way. I don't know. In a way that I feel saturated with American history and culture, and this is really the only place that I can function OK.

But that said, I have been having a thought just this week—and it may be because I got an email from a guy asking this same question. So I was thinking about it in my off hours during the week, about exactly what kind of allegiance do you owe to your country? That may be a big question for some people. I'm not sure that you really do owe it a lot if your country is making a foolish spectacle of itself.

DC: I heard Garrison Keillor say something on the radio once about how emigration is the highest form of protest that you can give to your government, or your nation.

JHK: Yeah, and there are a lot of things that are going on in the USA that are pretty deplorable and are a pretty good reason to consider going someplace else.

DC: People ask me sometimes why I don't just pack it up and go to Europe, because I complain about a lot of the aspects of American life. I thought I was going to end up in Scotland at one point. I went there for a few months and kicked around and really took a good look at the place. I had a great time and saw a lot of things. But I did realize then that it just isn't my country. It's not my culture and I don't belong to it.

JHK: That's an interesting point, because I have spent some time in Great Britain, and Ireland too, where they speak English. I felt very dissociated from the culture there, that despite the fact that we could understand each other we were not alike at all.

DC: Yeah, different values, different collective cultural experiences have become a part of who I am. But your point about one's allegiance to a country is interesting. I'm very attached to upstate New York and its history, because it's where I'm from and where my people have been for a long time. What's interesting about this part of New York State is that it's been controlled by a handful of different nations in a relatively short period of history. I don't feel as strong of an allegiance to the nationality, of being an American, as I do to this part of this...

JHK: The land.

DC: Yeah, this land, and this ongoing story of the land and the people who inhabit it. My people have been kicking around this corner of the Earth for three hundred and fifty years. We fucked this place up in a lot of ways, and I feel obligated to stick it through. Does that sound crazy?

JHK: No. It's not unrelated to how I feel about it. There's one other element though, which was the one that H.L. Mencken spoke of in the 1920s.

People would always ask him, "If you think this county is so ridiculous, why don't you just go somewhere else?" His answer was, "This is the greatest show on earth, and I've got a front row seat as a journalist and as a commentator. I wouldn't miss it for the world."[1]

To some extent that's how I feel about this clusterfuck that we're all witnessing and that some of us are actively commenting on. I feel in a way I am like the Bob Costas of the clusterfuck, giving blow-by-blow commentary on what's going on. So for me it is kind of amusing. Although I must say I'm a little bit daunted by the potential for trouble and danger. I'm not very paranoid, but I start seeing these nuts coming out at the health care town meetings, and the Sarah Palinites and the Mike Huckabees and the sort of corn-pone Nazis, and I'm not kidding about that. It is a joke in a way, but it's a serious joke. I think that there's tremendous potential in this country for political despotism and total looniness.

It really makes me quake in my boots to imagine those people getting their hands on the levers of power. It's not that wild to imagine that it could happen if the people in this country go through enough hardship and distress, which they seem to be heading into. It does seem to me that the US economy is still unraveling as much as it was in early 2009, that the recovery that's supposedly going on is a mirage, and that we're going to see a lot more mischief in banking and finance and the economy in general, and job loss and foreclosure and all the things that we're now familiar with. These are trends that you can't really see the horizon on.

So if I were a twenty-five-year-old who spoke French and had some gold overseas and had some ambitions to maybe buy some land and do some farming in Europe, that might not be such a bad idea.

Cassandra

Duncan Crary: You're sometimes called a Cassandra.

James Howard Kunstler: And that's a negative term, because it refers to somebody who's issuing warnings that nobody takes seriously and nobody wants to listen to.

DC: But Cassandra from Greek mythology, she *knew* the future. The problem was that nobody would listen to her.

JHK: That's true.

DC: At least you get credited for being right, even if no one listens to you.

JHK: I guess. George M. Cohan: "I'd rather be right than be president." So there you go.

DC: Of course we won't know if you were a Cassandra or—

JHK: Just a pure fake, a mountebank, a charlatan.

DC: —or not, until the future arrives. Sometimes I fantasize about traveling back to 1946 America to warn of the dangers to come from suburbanizing this country, and to persuade the country against it… Even in my dreams I can't stop it from happening!

JHK: I'm not sure that it's really possible to persuade people who get into a certain groove at a certain time in history. Their behavior is much more controlled by whatever things are easily at hand, and whatever materials and ideas are current at the time. That's pretty much what governs people's lives. Sometimes whole societies make unfortunate decisions or go down tragic pathways. Suburbia was ours.

Peering Into Yesterday's Tomorrow

JHK: Somebody sent me one of those wonderful illustrations that I collect of "The City of the Future," drawn in 1925. It was explicitly New York. It was a cross section of Park Avenue going underground about four levels, where they had rationally put all of the service infrastructure underground, including the automobile corridors.

The thing that amazed me about it was how wonderfully rational it all was. The streets were quite nice. There were no cars up on Park Avenue, as there are now. This was the city of the future. In fact they were quite precise about the date, which was 1925 doing a picture of 1950. You had the subway. So you had public transit on level three. You had the cars in these underground boulevards on level two. You had some other stuff on the first basement level. And ultimately way down below, you had the water mains and the electric lines and all that stuff.

DC: And the Morlocks below that.

JHK: Yeah, well, they didn't go above that. But what amazed me was the rationality of it all. Human beings are wonderfully intelligent and rational animals. If you put somebody down at a drawing board and a computer and you ask them to visually describe the perfect urban organism, they're smart enough to come up with these wonderful systems and these wonderful ways of doing things. But the trouble is, even though we can do the schematic, diagrammatic plans, we can't necessarily make them come out that way.

Human life is very sketchy and dodgy and imperfect and impromptu. It's interrupted by all kinds of fiascoes and blunders and disasters that sometimes can go on for decades or centuries, and an awful lot of stuff doesn't work out. Because life is really emergent and self-organizing and fractal and chaotic. It just doesn't move that way. As soon as you believe you've solved one problem, the solution itself becomes a problem.

So now in our time, it's really a question of what's going to be happening next. I'm serenely convinced that what we're going to see from now on is going to be largely an impromptu thing. People are going to be making stuff up as they go along. Because we're mostly going to be using leftover materials, leftover buildings, leftover salvaged stuff that we're going to put things together with. I'm quite sure we'll do good work with it, just as the people in the

Middle Ages did with what Rome left over.

Maybe the people after them will do better. It does present tremendous opportunities for young people, who may not know it because their whole experience has been suburban so far. But a lot of their lives are actually going to be taking place very differently. They're coming out of college with maybe no idea of what the shape and texture of life is going to be for their adulthood. I think it isn't going to be with an experience in the suburban utopia of our time.

But it's going to be impromptu, and it's going to be emergent, and it's going to be not quite exactly what we all expect. And I'm kind of excited about it, because this whole modernity has been extremely tiresome for me. I don't even like the costumes we wear anymore. I want to wear a sword.

Legacy

DC: Have you ever thought about the legacy that you're going to leave behind? Do you ever think about how you want to be remembered or what you want your contribution to be?
JHK: I haven't thought about it in those terms, exactly. The way I think about anything remotely like that, is that I'm comfortable with what I've accomplished in my life—I can look at a shelf of books and say, "Hey, I wrote a shelf of books." So I know that I didn't go through this world uselessly for the time that I took up.

I'm fairly comfortable with who I turned out to be as an adult human being. I actually did learn how to take care of myself after a pretty bad start in adulthood, a floundering start of not even being able to pay the light bill. I finally figured that out.

My matrimonial record's a bit sketchy, and not something I'm really proud of—I apologize to all of my ex-wives and even some girlfriends. I didn't have any children. It just worked out that way despite the fact that I was married and did perform the procreative act more than a few times.

Probably the only thing I'm really kind of sorry about is that I didn't dress better. I work at home so I can just put any old thing on and go to my office. I kind of wish—I mean I would want to go the Tom Wolfe route. I have a fantasy about old Tom, whom I only met once in my whole life in an elevator. My fantasy about Tom is that he's living in some kind of an East Side townhouse, and he gets up every morning and puts on a white suit and goes to a beautifully appointed office with like a Louis Quatorze antique desk that probably costs $104,000 with all kinds of inlaid marquetry. And he's there in his white suit with a handkerchief in his white suit pocket and some kind of a beautiful Hermès tie, you know, and he looks great. And then he rolls out of his office and goes out to lunch at a place where people see him in his white suit and they say, "Oh he's wearing a white suit. He looks very nice." I'm kind of sorry that I don't do that—that I'm just wearing my old Polartec velour zip-up full of cat hair.

So I apologize to you, Duncan, because I could have put on better clothes for you. Maybe next year my New Year's resolution will be that "I'm going to put on a tie when he comes over to do the podcast or if I go down to his crib in Troy and do it there."

Outro

"It takes the silence of a town like Troy to stir the mind."
—Richard Selzer, *Down From Troy*

TEN YEARS AGO I moved to Troy, New York, a small American city of exactly the type James Howard Kunstler sees prospering in the new energy future. There's no denying that the place is struggling now, and has been for the better half of a century. But I am confident that its many underutilized features will be valued once again as events unfold. These assets include a tight network of walkable streets and blocks; a major inland water route; access to passenger rail; and an abrupt transition to nearby farmlands, with few suburban intrusions. For the most part, my life here even resembles the kind of scaled-down existence that Jim envisions for people of the future.

All of this has served as a great backdrop and Petri dish for our ongoing conversations about urbanism and the Long Emergency. But I am not in Troy living the way I am out of any concerns or preparations for a post-peak oil world. I am here because I want to be here—now—and because I find it deeply rewarding to be in this place, in spite of its long-festering state. Life is charming for me here, in and amongst the residue of nineteenth-century industrial wealth. Even on my tight income, I never find myself locked out from any luxuries, although it helps that I'm easily amused and fairly modest in my tastes. My neighborhood is my living room, office, playground and marketplace, and I seldom need or even desire to leave.

My days are punctuated by design with dozens of inefficient chores, which wind me around the blocks in and out of the stores and offices far more times than logic demands. I make these trips on foot for the simple pleasure of being immersed in a beautifully designed urban fabric, and for the inevitable encounters with friends, neighbors and clients along the way. Why buy groceries in bulk when I can walk to the co-op and chat with the clerks each morning? Evenings I often spend bouncing on foot from one pub to the next, where I am always in the company of good friends or gregarious strangers. No need to call or text first before setting out—I know I'll never be alone, unless I choose to be.

At the moment I still own a car, but rarely ever use it except to drive to Saratoga to talk with Jim about suburban sprawl and fossil fuel depletion. The irony of that does not elude me. I do take the occasional road trip. More often I'll ride the train to New York City or Burlington. I enjoy being in nature as much as any other "outdoorsman." But even the places for those activities can be reached without a car. There are plenty of swimming holes, canoe launches, campsites, bike paths and hiking trails along the periphery of town. I visit them often.

All of this might lead one to surmise that I am ignorant of or antagonistic toward the world at large. But I have seen and lived in other parts of it. I imagine I will again. For now, I find great satisfaction in the daily rhythms of life within this small sphere. And it's exciting to see the place gradually shake off its atrophy. Our city leaders are incrementally repairing and replacing the missing teeth along our streets, correcting mistakes from a less thoughtful era. There are fits and starts and temper tantrums along the way. I'm sure there will be more. Overall, though, these efforts are progressing, and I'm pleased to witness them from the front row.

And I'm not deluded—we still have a long way to go before the place can be described as bustling. There are many more empty buildings and vacant lots yet to be occupied by businesses or residents. Our public image needs improving, too. The suburbanites still hold wildly exaggerated notions about the crime, the bad schools and the lack of parking in our allegedly narrow streets. But even they are starting to poke around more frequently, for our farmers' markets, our bar scene and our festivals. At this point, they still need to be bribed with gimmicks and special events in order to arrive in large numbers. It is funny, however, how the most popular of these festivals are centered on walking, shopping and dining in our quaint downtown. After all, these late-night Fridays and weekend fairs are really just dressed-up versions of what people normally do every weekend with a healthy city: use it. It's baffling that people need a contrived invitation to come visit, and the situation used to frustrate me, until Kunstler helped calm my impatience by describing these activities as "American society rehearsing for the era to come," when we will once again walk, shop and revel in the places where we live and work. That gives me a lot of hope.

I really do find much to be optimistic about in Jim's forecast, in spite of his reputation for being a "doomer." I feel indebted to him for that because it's often difficult for me to stay positive about the direction we're moving as a culture. As an upstate New Yorker, I am constantly reminded by our grand rotting cities that better days are behind us. Our landscape is littered with crumbling edifices and weed-choked manufacturing centers. Our pre-automobile transit systems are buried under tarmac, or rusting out in the sun or lost in the woods. When I come across these visible reminders of abandoned enterprise, I find it hard to imagine that I am descended from the same people who created them. The people of my time, for the most part, have little affection for our historic infrastructure and dwelling places, preferring to sprawl out into the ChemLawn hinterlands instead. They choose particleboard and plastic over brick and stone. They prefer asphalt to Belgian block. They favor parking lots and driveways over walkable neighborhoods and public transit. They find corporate-controlled transactions more convenient than independent commerce. And so on.

Economically, the region has been bust for generations. Many of our most talented young minds flee after school for employment in Manhattan, Boston or the Sunbelt. This has been the backdrop of my life. Yet I choose to stay because the place speaks to me and I am haunted by thoughts that these trends could be reversed—that these buildings and cities and elegant means of moving between them could be resurrected. I often fantasize that I could have lived here in the earlier, car-free and lively days. But talking with Jim over the years has given me reason to hope that I may see some form of that world return in my lifetime. What else can I say other than I am so very grateful to have been shown that glimpse of a more satisfying future? Grateful for the hours he gave me to interact with him personally, professionally and consistently.

When we set out on this adventure in podcasting, I never imagined we would still be at it four years later. By my count, I have now spent the equivalent of seventy-eight days around the clock with Kunstler's words beaming directly into my ears. And that's just the time I have devoted to recording, editing and producing our weekly conversations. There were additional months spent poring over his published books, and the transcripts of our conversations that formed the basis of this publication. I sometimes relate the experience to being an embedded reporter: Kunstler was my source and beat for four whole years. When you spend that much time with a source, you form a bond and perhaps even a friendship. In my case, I seem to have developed intellectual Stockholm Syndrome, for which I have no plans to seek counseling.

During our time together, we spoke at length about specific cities and places around the world, as well as current events, rock 'n' roll, hunting, porn, space exploration. We examined the finer points of building to the human scale, public art, urban thinkers—even paving materials. Our conversation overflowed onto the streets of Saratoga Springs, Troy and Rochester, New York. We talked in parks and on wild urban outcrops and even in a suburban shopping mall. When we couldn't get there in person, we explored Paris, Detroit and Baltimore virtually with Google's Street View program. More recently, we have invited other guests onto the show to contribute. I recorded far more content than I could include in these pages. But for the time being, all of those conversations are available for listening at KunstlerCast.com, where you can also find a list of important books and resources to learn more about these topics.

If I were strictly a journalist, I would probably be signing off differently with these parting words. But this project has always been something more than reporting or interviewing. From the start, I approached it as an odd apprenticeship of sorts. Our proximity, the timing and this emerging media form brought me together with Jim. It was a lucky happenstance for me that I was able to spend a great deal of time listening to and learning from one of the important minds of our era. I say that knowing full well that Kunstler is not a mainstream intellectual. He is a voice from the margins, where he chooses to thrive. But what he taught me during our time together is no less relevant to the mainstream today than it was eighteen years ago when *The Geography of Nowhere* was first published. I believe that I have absorbed a fair amount of information while bringing that voice to a few new ears and eyes. That alone is compensation enough for the work.

All apprenticeships must eventually come to an end, though, and this one is not exempt from the rule. And while I don't intend to ever stop talking with JHK, there will come a day soon—it's on the horizon—when we will unplug our microphones and move on to other projects. I know I still have a great deal left to learn. But already I find I have much to say on the destiny of my small corner of civilization, and I now feel better equipped to contribute to that discussion. I feel compelled to do so, in my own voice and way. It's clear even now that the culture I have known and battled with my whole life is fading. As it dies off, new opportunities will present themselves. I don't fear these changes. I welcome them, with serene confidence that the journey from here to there will be rewarding.

We certainly have our work cut out for us in my neck of the woods. But I think we'll get where we need to go. I imagine that you and your people will get to wherever you need to go as well, wherever that is. I look forward to seeing you on the other side.

I'm your host, Duncan Crary. Thanks for reading.

Notes

Chapter 1: The Geography of Nowhere

1. James Howard Kunstler, *The Geography of Nowhere*, (New York: Simon & Shuster, 1993) 10.

2. Kunstler said this in 2002, about the new-at-the-time MVP Health Care headquarters on State Street in Schenectady, New York. He was a featured speaker at the "Livable Cities" series, sponsored by the Schenectady Heritage Foundation, which I happened to be covering as a reporter for a small weekly newspaper, *The Journal*. See also Mike Fricano, "Critic Slams MVP Building," *Albany Times Union*, Monday, April 8, 2002, B1.

3. This is a line of dialogue spoken by the character Nell in Samuel Beckett's one-act play "Endgame," which premiered in 1957.

4. TED2004, "James H. Kunstler dissects suburbia," ted.com (accessed May 8, 2011).

5. John Morrissey was a street brawler from Troy, New York, who became a prizefighter nicknamed "Old Smoke." His connections to Tammany Hall scored him a brief stint in Congress, while his casino in Saratoga Springs, New York earned him a fortune. But after Morrissey returned to his hometown a wealthy and powerful man, his hopes of building a mansion in Troy's exclusive Washington Park neighborhood were dashed when the elitist property owners refused to sell him a plot. They just wouldn't stand for a man of such ill repute living amongst them in their wealthy, industrialist enclave. So the old street tough got revenge for the snub by building a horrid-smelling soap factory just close enough to his rivals' homes to make life rather unpleasant for their olfactories when the wind blew. See George Waller, *Saratoga: Saga of an Impious Era* (New York: Bonanza Books, 1966), 119–141.

6. Kunstler, *The Geography of Nowhere*, 114.

7. Ibid. 113.

8. See Chapter 2 of this book for a detailed discussion of the New Urbanisim.

9. Tom Wolfe, *From Bauhaus to Our House* (New York: Farrar, Straus & Giroux, 1981): "Every child goes to school in a building that looks like a duplicating-machine replacement-parts wholesale distribution warehouse.... Every new $900,000 summer house in the north woods of Michigan or on the shore of Long Island has so many pipe railings, ramps, hob-tread metal spiral stairways, sheets of industrial plate glass, banks of tungsten-halogen lamps, and white cylindrical shapes, it looks like an insecticide refinery."

   Incidentally, the Maple Ave. Middle School on Route 9 in Saratoga Springs made international news when security confiscated the bike of a twelve-year-old boy because bicycling to school was not permitted. The principal cited safety concerns over traffic and lack of supervision, although the boy's mother had cycled into school with him. She was instructed to return by car to pick up her child and his bike. See Andrew J. Bernstein, "Student's Bike Ride Earns Punishment," *The Saratogian*, May 23, 2009.

10. The estate that belonged to Charles Mackay was called Harbor Hill. The exterior of the house mimicked a French castle while the interior was decorated by the prestigious architectural firm Mc-Kim, Mead & White. The house burned in the 1940s. See Constance M. Grieff, *Lost America: From the Atlantic to the Mississippi* (Princeton: Pyne Press, 1971) and mackayhistory.com/HarborHill.html (accessed May 8, 2011).

11. Fritz Steiner and Talia McCray, "We Knew It All Along," *Planning*, July 2009.

12. Thomas E. Rinaldi and Robert J. Yasinsac, *Hudson Valley Ruins: Forgotten Landmarks of an American Landscape* (Hanover: University Press of New England, 2006), 1.

13. Kunstler, *The Geography of Nowhere*, 40–41.

14. *Crumb*, 1995 documentary. Sony Pictures Classic Directed by Terry Zwigoff, produced by Lynn O'Donnell.

15. Robert Crumb and Peter Poplaski, *The R. Crumb Handbook* (London: MQ Publications, 2005), 18.

16. Robert Bruegmann, *Sprawl: A Compact History* (Chicago: University of Chicago Press, 2005). For Kunstler's review of this book, see *Salmagundi* (Fall 2006, No. 152).

17. Darrell Huff, *How to Lie with Statistics* (New York: Norton, 1954).

18. For example, Randal O'Toole, the self-proclaimed "antiplanner," is a senior fellow with the Cato Institute, a libertarian think tank founded by oil conglomerate

Koch Industries leaders Edward H. Crane and Charles Koch.

19. Kunstler participated in a structured debate with O'Toole at Brown University in April 2010. A video of the debate, titled "Building America: Who should Control Urban Growth?", appears online at YouTube (accessed May 8, 2011).

20. Joel Kotkin is a distinguished presidential fellow in Urban Futures at Chapman University in Orange, California, and an adjunct fellow with the Legatum Institute, a think tank based in London, UK. He is the author of *The New Geography: How the Digital Revolution Is Reshaping the American Landscape* (New York: Random House, 2002).

21. David Brooks, "Relax, We'll Be Fine," *The New York Times*, April 5, 2010.

22. David Brooks, *Bobos in Paradise: The New Upper Class And How They Got There* (New York: Simon & Shuster, 2000).

23. "All truth passes through three stages. First, it is ridiculed. Second, it is violently opposed. Third, it is accepted as being self-evident," —Arthur Schopenhauer, German philosopher (1788–1860).

24. James Howard Kunstler, "How To Mess Up a Town," *Planning Commissioners Journal*, issue 17 (Winter 1995).

25. Michael Kinsley, "The Least We Can Do, " *The Atlantic*, October 2010.

Chapter 2: The End of Suburbia

1. FDR's Servicemen's Readjustment Act of 1944 (a.k.a. the G.I. Bill of Rights) provided low-interest, zero-down-payment home loans for servicemen.

2. Marcus Vitruvius Pollio was a Roman writer, architect and engineer in the first century BCE. He is best known as the author of the multi-volume work *De Architectura* ("On Architecture").

3. Werner Hegemann and Elbert Peets, *The American Vitruvius: An Architects' Handbook of Civic Art* (New York: The Architectural Book Publishing Company, 1922).

4. Page 253

5. Kunstler, *The Geography of Nowhere*, 253.

6. See: "Remarks by the President on America's Energy Security," Georgetown University, March 30, 2011, m.whitehouse. gov/the-press-office/2011/03/30/remarks -president-americas-energy-security (accessed May 8, 2011) and Larry Kudlow, "The Kudlow Report," CNBC, March 23, 2011.

7. *The Knickerbocker News* was an evening newspaper covering Albany, New York. It was purchased in 1960 by the Hearst

Corporation, which also owned the competing *Albany Times Union* newspaper. Hearst discontinued *The Knickerbocker News* in 1988, but continues to publish *The Times Union* today. Its headquarters, where Kunstler worked, are at the end of Wolf Road, a commercial shopping strip in the suburban town of Colonie, New York.

8. Kunstler, *The Geography of Nowhere*, 47. Another example appears on page 114: "Americans are doing almost nothing to prepare for the end of the romantic dream that was the American automobile age."

9. James Howard Kunstler, "My Y2K—A Personal Statement" (April 1999), kunstler.com/mags_y2k.html (accessed May 8, 2011).

10. Others who are also lumped into the category of "doomer" include Dmitry Orlov, *Reinventing Collapse*; John Michael Greer, *The Long Descent*; Jay Hanson, DieOff.com; and James Lovelock, "The Gaia Theory."

11. James Howard Kunstler, *The Long Emergency* (New York: Grove/Atlantic, 2005), 18.

Chapter 3: American Culture

1. "This book seeks to indentify those failures, and it necessarily contains a good measure of ridicule, which is the inescapable fate of the ridiculous," Kunstler, *Home from Nowhere*, 18.

2. US Energy Information Administration.

3. See: James Howard Kunstler, "Eyesore of the Month," August 2008 kunstler.com/eyesore_200808.html and "The Coming Re-Becoming," Clusterfuck Nation, July 28, 2008 kunstler.com/mags_diary24.html (accessed May 8, 2011).

4. The Third Place is a term for community spaces where people interact and socialize, such as bars and cafés. The First Place is the home; the Second Place is the workspace.

Chapter 4: Architecture

1. The Experimental Media & Performance Arts Center, or EMPAC, was designed by Nicholas Grimshaw: www.empac.rpi.edu/building (accessed May 8, 2011). Architectural critic William Morgan described it as maybe the "most outrageous…building to appear in upstate New York in decades." See William Morgan "Beached Ocean Liner in Troy," *The Providence Journal*, May 4, 2009.

2. The State University of New York, Brockport.

3. *The Haus der Kulturen der Welt* (House of World Cultures) is also known to Berliners as the Schwangere Auster ("The Pregnant Oyster").

4. Barbara Bradley Hagerty, "Future Of Brutalist-Designed Church Not Concrete," NPR, August 21, 2008. See also: Sarah Abruzzese, "Church Sues Over Landmark Status," *The New York Times*, August 7, 2008.

Chapter 5: Getting There

1. According to a 2008 report on consumer expenditures in 2006, the US Department of Labor's US Bureau of Labor Statistics found that the average cost to own and maintain a car in America is $8,003. The breakdown includes $3,421 to purchase the car, $2,227 for gas and oil, and $2,355 in other related costs. AAA puts the average annual cost of owning a car at $9,641, and those calculations were based on an average gas cost of $2.256 per gallon. See Lisa Smith, "The True Cost Of Owning A Car," *Investopedia*, July 11, 2008.

2. "Slugging" is the term for semiformal, anonymous carpooling in Washington, D.C., and other cities with major traffic congestion and high-occupancy vehicle lanes that incentivize driving with more passengers. There are a few versions of where the name came from.

3. The Chicago Sanitary and Ship Canal is the only commercial shipping link between the Great Lakes System and the Mississippi River System. It replaced The Illinois and Michigan Canal.

Chapter 6: The City in Mind

1. David Owen "Green Manhattan: Everywhere Should be More Like New York," *The New Yorker*, October 18, 2004.

2. The panel discussion "Manhattan: the Greenest Place in America" took place at the National Arts Club on October 20, 2009, and featured David Owen; James Howard Kunstler; Gary Brewer, an architect with Robert A.M. Stern; and Paul Stoller, a sustainability consultant who is director of environmental design consultants Atelier Ten.

3. See David Streitfeld, "An Effort to Save Flint, Mich., by Shrinking It," *The New York Times*, April 21, 2009; and Belinda Lanks, "Creative Shrinkage," *The New York Times*, December 10, 2006.

4. On the band's final album, *Naked*, released in 1988.

5. This 1993 movie, starring Daniel Day-Lewis and Michelle Pfeiffer, was based on the historical novel by Edith Wharton from 1920, set in New York City in the 1870s.

6. "My City Was Gone" by the Pretenders, released in 1982 as a b-side to the hit single "Back On the Chain Gang."

7. Section 8 is a federal housing voucher program provided by the United States Department of Housing and Urban Development (HUD) which subsidizes housing costs for low-income families and individuals.

8. Co-op City, or "Cooperative City," is located in the Bronx and dates back to the 1960s

and early '70s. It consists of more than than thirty residential high-rise towers surrounded by "green spaces."

9. Trevanian, *The Crazyladies of Pearl Street* (New York: Crown, 2005), 13.

10. The Jevons paradox is an observation that whenever technology makes it possible to use a resource more efficiently, it usually leads to a greater consumption rate of that same resource. Kunstler usually talks about the paradox in terms of fossil fuel usage.

Chapter 7: Urban Polemicists

1. During a campaign stop in Ohio on August 31, 2008, Barack Obama referred to Jacobs' *The Death and Life of Great American Cities* as "a great book." A video of this exchange posted to YouTube was widely circulated by New Urbanists. See Bill Dawers, "City Talk: Back to basics with Jane Jacobs," *Savanah Morning News*, January 6, 2009.

2. James Howard Kunstler, "Godmother of the American City," *Metropolis Magazine*, March 2001.

3. The 1939 World's Fair was held in New York City and included an exhibit and ride called Futurama. Sponsored by General Motors, it predicted what the world would be like twenty years later, with things like automated highways and endless suburbs.

4. "On the fringe of mass suburbia, even the advantages of the primary neighborhood group disappear. The cost of this detachment in space from other men is out of all proportion to its supposed benefits. The end product is an encapsulated life, spent more and more either in a motor car or within the cabin of darkness before a television set." Lewis Mumford, *The City in History: Its Origins, Its Transformations, and Its Prospects* (New York: Harcourt, Brace and World, 1961), 512. Quoted in Kunstler, *The Geography of Nowhere*, 10.

Chapter 8: Parting Words

1. "All the while I have been forgetting the third of my reasons for remaining so faithful a citizen of the Federation, despite all the lascivious inducements from expatriates to follow them beyond the seas, and all the surly suggestions from patriots that I succumb. It is the reason which grows out of my mediaeval but unashamed taste for the bizarre and indelicate, my congenital weakness for comedy of the grosser varieties. The United States, to my eye, is incomparably the greatest show on earth." H.L. Mencken, "On Being an American," from *Prejudices, Third Series* (New York: Alfred A. Knopf, 1922), 57–58.

Index

Index

About the Contributors

Cal Crary

Duncan Crary is host and producer of The KunstlerCast, a talkshow podcast featuring author James Howard Kunstler. He has also recorded face-to-face podcast interviews with many notable personalities, including Sir Salman Rushdie, E.O. Wilson and Christopher Hitchens. He has worked as a reporter for newspapers and magazines, and was a founding editor of *Salvage*, a newsprint magazine of literature and art.

He lives in Troy, New York, where he is self-employed as a publicist and new media consultant. He plans to launch a new podcast series based on life in a small American city in 2012. His website is DuncanCrary.com.

James Howard Kunstler is the author of *The Geography of Nowhere, The City in Mind, Home from Nowhere* and *The Long Emergency*, as well as eleven novels, including *World Made*

By Hand and *The Witch of Hebron*. He is currently finishing his next nonfiction book, which examines the diminishing returns of technology. His writing has also appeared in *The New York Times Magazine*, *The Washington Post*, *The Atlantic Monthly*, *Metropolis*, *Rolling Stone*, *Playboy* and many other periodicals.

Kunstler was born in New York City in 1948 and has lived in Saratoga Springs, New York, for more than thirty years. His website, where he publishes his popular *Clusterfuck Nation* blog every Monday, is Kunstler.com.

Ken Avidor is an artist in Minneapolis, Minnesota. His anti-car comic strip "Roadkill Bill" was published weekly in *Pulse of the Twin Cities* and reprinted in *Carbusters*, *Auto-Free Times* and other environmental and anti-car publications. An excerpt from his forthcoming graphic novel *Bicyclopolis* appears in *Cifiscape vol. I: The Twin Cities*, published by Onyx Neon. Avidor's website is AvidorStudios.com.

BETTER TOWNS, CITIES, PLACES. BETTER DESIGN, HEALTH, LIVING.
A BETTER CNU.

CNU

Join the Congress for the New Urbanism
and become part of the movement to create
compact, vibrant, engaging, and better-
performing neighborhoods at every scale.

Go to **www.cnu.org/membership**

If you have enjoyed *The KunstlerCast*, you might also enjoy other

BOOKS TO BUILD A NEW SOCIETY

Our books provide positive solutions for people who want to
make a difference. We specialize in:

**Sustainable Living • Green Building • Peak Oil • Renewable Energy
Environment & Economy • Natural Building & Appropriate Technology
Progressive Leadership • Resistance & Community • Educational & Parenting Resources**

New Society Publishers

ENVIRONMENTAL BENEFITS STATEMENT

New Society Publishers has chosen to produce this book on recycled paper made with **100%
post consumer waste,** processed chlorine free, and old growth free.
For every 5,000 books printed, New Society saves the following resources:[1]

21	Trees
1,921	Pounds of Solid Waste
2,113	Gallons of Water
2,757	Kilowatt Hours of Electricity
3,492	Pounds of Greenhouse Gases
15	Pounds of HAPs, VOCs, and AOX Combined
5	Cubic Yards of Landfill Space

[1]Environmental benefits are calculated based on research done by the Environmental Defense Fund and
other members of the Paper Task Force who study the environmental impacts of the paper industry.

For a full list of NSP's titles, please call 1-800-567-6772 *or check out our website* at:

www.newsociety.com

NEW SOCIETY PUBLISHERS